Also by Regena Thomashauer

Mama Gena's School of Womanly Arts

Mama Gena's Owner's and Operator's Guide to Men

Regena Thomashauer

Simon & Schuster

New York   London   Toronto   Sydney   Singapore

SIMON & SCHUSTER
Rockefeller Center
1230 Avenue of the Americas
New York, NY 10020

SIMON & SCHUSTER and colophon are registered trademarks
of Simon & Schuster, Inc.

For information regarding special discounts for bulk purchases, please contact Simon &
Schuster Special Sales at 1-800-456-6798 or business@simonandschuster.com

Designed by Jan Pisciotta

Manufactured in the United States of America

10   9   8   7   6   5   4   3   2   1

Library of Congress Cataloging-in-Publication Data
Thomashauer, Regena.
Mama Gena's owners's and operator's guide to men / Regena Thomashauer.
p. cm.
1. Man-woman relationships. 2. Interpersonal relations.   I. Title.
HQ801.T453 2003
306.7—dc21
2003045537

ISBN 0-7432-4798-1

This book is dedicated to all the men who have had the courage, despite the obstacles, to love women, to listen to women, and to prioritize women.

This book is dedicated to women who, despite the obstacles, are willing to be fully and completely themselves, to bring men into their world, and to love them.

Acknowledgments

Thank you Bruce, my best friend, for joining me on this grand research experiment that is our magnificent life, together.

To our man-training expert, our daughter, Maggie Rose, who makes sure she gets everything she wants, to our great joy.

Thank you, Vera and Steve Bodansky, for fueling my jets with my own passion, and for living a gloriously fulfilled life with one another so I could learn how.

Thank you, Lydia, Joan, and Kate, but especially Lyd, for insisting we remain friends for twenty-five years, and for sharing the wonderful, the tragic, the silly, the reverential, and the irreverential in our lives together. The gift of our friendship has been a creative cornerstone for me, since we met as teenagers. I am so grateful.

To my mom, for her loyalty, love, and perspective on life. A moment will come in my day, every day, where I just want to talk to my mother. I feel so grateful that I can pick up the phone and there she is.

To my dad, who was there as I cut my man-training teeth, and who always, somehow, eventually ended up saying "yes!" to my desires.

To my mother and father by marriage, Rita and the late Howard Thomashauer, who gave me the greatest gift of all, their son, Bruce.

Thank you to Bryan Bradley and Amanda Cutter Brooks, for the clothes, the style, the hot, throbbing fashion of it all.

Thank you, Lori Sutherland and Deborah Lack Daniels, for your presence and your courage, and for the joy of working with you each day.

Thank you, J.B. and Laura, for our beautiful friendship and for your inspiring, fun, hot relationship with each other.

Thanks to Glenn and Christina, for introducing me to Dr. Vic Baranco and the other master teachers at More. Thank you for the magnificent, soul-altering education.

Thank you to my agent, Jen Gates, a gorgeous human being, a powerhouse businesswoman, and a literary genius. Thank you for always going that extra mile with me.

A hallelujah chorus of thanks to my gorgeous, passionate, brilliant editor, Amanda Murray, who, with her rapier wit and incisive vision, lifts me to aspects of my genius that would be unavailable without her.

Thank you to Starbucks, especially the gang at 87th and Broadway, and especially that leather chair in the window, where I greeted the dawn for many months. Thank you for welcoming writers and laptops and playing great music.

Thank you, Martha McCully and Katie Brown, for your inspiration.

And to Bing Brown, my swashbuckling lawyer, who takes exquisite care of me.

Author's Note

The stories about people told in this book reflect feelings or situations which many of us have experienced in our own lives. While the essence of the stories is real, many are composites and, in most cases, names of individuals and other characteristics have been changed.

Contents

Mama Gena's
Owner's and Operator's
Guide to Men

Introduction

Darlings, darlings, darlings, have no fear, Mama Gena is here! Here to take you high and make you fly and have your way with the men in this world. My darlings, I want you to feel the same kind of navigational certainty with your men as you do when you slip behind the steering wheel of your car or assemble the ingredients for your favorite recipe or organize a conference at work. I want you to know your way, with confidence, over that terrain called "men." I want you to become the navigatrix you were born to be. I want you to feel every drop of exquisite power and beauty and gloriousness that you, as women, were designed to feel in relationships with men.

I am so over your sacrificing yourselves and diminishing yourselves and belittling yourselves. I am done, done, done, I tell you, with tales of women doing things to make other people happy, at the expense of themselves. And I want you to be done, too. Or at least, if not done, then open to the idea that things can get a whole lot better than they are. And how do they get better, Mama? They get better, so better, fantastically, unbelievably better, when we, as women, take control of the steering wheel and begin to own and operate our men, and own and operate ourselves.

I want you all to have the unprecedented experience of true partnership with the men in your lives. You cannot be partners with

someone you are subservient to. You can't be partners with someone you are obligated to. Partnership is a game of equals, each playing their different part. A knife and a fork are equals, but different.
Men and women are equals, but different. When we know our part
and play it to the maximum effect, and guys know and play their
part to the maximum effect, it is a fantastic combination. A union of
differences! Which translates to the thing we want the most—a
friendship in which intimacy and closeness and fun grow over a lifetime. I want you each to relish your womanhood and relish the deliciousness of your relationships with men. Mama wants you to have
a man who serves you, worships you, and adores you. A sex life that
is constantly evolving, expanding, and giving you extended, massive
pleasure. A deep, lovely friendship with a guy who is on your side
and wants you to have everything you desire. A partner. A best
friend you have sex with. Why would any sane woman want anything less? Ultimately, I want you to be capable of creating a partnership with another human being that reflects you, enhances you,
and brings you and your partner the kind of intimacy and ecstasy
that you long for, and probably don't see many examples of in the
world. My life's work has been about that journey.

Let us reinvent the path to succulent, joyous relationships.
Don't you want to get it so good that all of your girlfriends want
what you have? Mama is here to pose and answer the question
"What is it, exactly, that we are supposed to *do* with men?" She
will explain why the time has finally come for women to fulfill
their destiny: owning and operating men. It is a tough job, oh Sister Goddesses, but someone's gotta do it.

By the time you finish reading this book, you'll be able to grab the steering wheel and own and operate your men. All of your men. Your husbands, fathers, boyfriends, dry cleaners, brothers, bosses, employees, waiters, gardeners, and hairdressers. Go get 'em, gals, they are there purely for your pleasure.

At this point, I have a warning and a request: This book is by a woman, for women only. This book simply is not for men. I teach a whole wonderful course for men called "Mama Gena Gives It Up to Men." And do I ever. But this is not that. This is Mama, speaking to her sisters, and if you are a guy, you may feel offended or diminished or slighted. And that is not my goal. I adore men. I love the way they feel, the way they smell, the way they melt me with love and make me weak in the knees. I love to surrender to their touch and feel them respond to mine. I am grateful for their loyalty, their adoration, and their steadfast devotion. But this is not "giving it up to men" time. This is "giving it up to my Sister Goddesses" time.

A Sister Goddess is a woman who has taken one of my courses or read one of my books. "Sister," because we as women are all sisters, and "Goddess" because every woman has a spark of the divine in her. And when you treat a woman as a sister and as a goddess, you bring out the best in her. And bringing out the best in a woman is a very brilliant thing to do. The goal of this book is exactly that—to bring out the divine in all of you. I have fantastic desires and dreams about women creating lives with their men that include an abundance of sensuality, fun, and intimate joy with each other. And my method is to exclude you, guys, and lay some truth on my Sisters.

Indulge Mama, would you? If you are a man, shut this book instantly. Return it to the shelf you took it from. Leave me alone with the ladies. It's time for a woman-to-woman chat. I'll get to you next time. Remember, Mama loves you. . . .

Now, my darling Sister Goddesses, you know that owning and operating men is something that has been going on for centuries, just as gravity had been going on for centuries before Newton drew it to our attention. Women have been in charge of men since the dawn of time. It is only now that we can articulate and gain control of that which has always existed. Before we knew there was gravity, some valuable piece of jewelry might have been carried off by the wind or floated away or vanished. Once we knew about gravity, we could take advantage of it, count on it, put our fears to rest. We know that missing jewels were either dropped, misplaced, stolen, or else exactly where we left them. We are in control because we understand how this unseen force affects our universe. The laws of owning and operating men work precisely the same way. Once we understand the laws, we are confident, we are in control, and we know what to do next. If he leaves you, it's not because you are a loser or because you are not worthy or that you will never hold on to a man. If he has left, it's because you were done with him, or he was poorly trained before you found him, or you are clearing the decks for something much better. There is method to the madness.

Now, Mama, you say that women have been in control of men since the dawn of time—what do you mean by that exactly? I believe that Helen had Paris by the balls, that Cleopatra gave eternity to Marc Antony and Julius Caesar, that greatness, inspiration, life, passion, creativity, new directions, innovations all come directly from the impact, influence, and presence of women.

I grew up in a world, like you did, where natural law seemed rather different. My father worked, my mother was responsible for the food and housekeeping. Cover story was that he made all the decisions; he was the head of the household. But I noticed that the most significant decisions in our family life originated from her, not him. We moved from one house to another when she decided she wanted a bigger one. There were three children because she wanted three. We got used cars because she thought new ones were a waste of money. My brothers became doctors because she wanted them to. And the only person her desire had no impact on was me, the only other female. I actually used to get quite annoyed at my dad for being so vulnerable to her power. Men were presidents, doctors, lawyers, and heads of newspapers, TV stations, magazines. They were God, basically, and yet I noticed my dad could not get out of the house in the morning without my mom picking out his clothes for him. A widely respected physician required help matching his tie to his shirt and would wear black socks and shoes to the beach with his bathing suit unless we stopped him.

And you know, the point I am making is not about fashion. It's about power and responsibility. It's about exposing exactly how things are and playing with the cards we are dealt, rather than playing with some already extinct, outdated models that won't lead to happiness. If we keep mimicking our parents' relationships, we will never get to experience the outrageous joy that is available in a game of equals, a game of partners.

Think of owning and operating men as simply an alternative experiment, darlings. The current experiment is an abysmal failure. You know, the whole women-serving-men thing, the whole he's-superior-and-we're-inferior thing. They don't like it, we don't like it. It's a disaster, really. Look at the divorce rate—50 percent of all marriages end in divorce, and it's 100 percent in the state of California because so many people get married and then divorce and then remarry and divorce and then marry again and divorce. One person with three divorces could be responsible for a 300 percent divorce rate. In New York City, 60 percent of all households are single. Why is that? And yet, women all over the world are stuffing themselves into long white gowns and scurrying down the aisle as though it were a blue light special at Kmart. What's up with that? If someone told you about a fabulous mutual fund you could invest in, and said that it might or might not give you any interest and that there was a 50 percent chance you could lose your whole investment, you know for a fact that you would decline the offer. So why are women rushing toward marriage with the same purposeful abandon as kamikaze pilots in World War II?

Why are we failing so miserably? In the last century, and in those before, one of the great driving goals of life was simple survival: food and shelter. Man was the provider and the woman supported him. The male-dominated relationship paradigm was great for survival of the human species. We are a living testament to its effectiveness. In order to survive, there needed to be a man going out to hunt or fish or gather, and a woman to tend the home and birth the babies. For the last five thousand years or so, women have traded sex, housekeeping, and childcare for food and shelter from male providers. Even now, many women put their needs behind those of their husbands. Happiness has not been considered a priority.

In the twenty-first century, in this country, we are privileged. Most of us have our survival handled, and we are free to pursue happiness. Once you have survival handled, the purpose of life changes. In this country we are promised, "life, liberty, and the pursuit of happiness." These days, the common goal for individuals and relationships is happiness. Each of us can handle the survival stuff on our own. What we want with each other is more happiness than we can create alone. We lack the skills needed to create great, fabulous, fun relationships that start well and get better and better over a lifetime. We were taught how to "do" relationships by people who created bonds for survival purposes. For our grandparents, happiness was not a goal; food, shelter, and reproduction were their priorities. We're working with an outdated blueprint: the relationship equivalent of trying to fly to the moon in a 747.

Or doing microsurgery with a machete. You can't reach your goals unless you use the right instrument.

Mama will reveal an entirely new model for relationships: the Sister Goddess model, one that is in sync with the men and women of today. The Sister Goddess paradigm is what will take us to our new goals: pleasurable survival, or the creation of fun, intimacy, happiness, gratitude, celebration, and joy. True friendships between men and women are the new opportunity of this century. This book will be a blueprint for how to successfully create a relationship of true friendship and genuine intimacy. That thing that everyone wants but no one has a clue how to get. You know this world is hungry for some new ideas. And ain't it the truth that if you want to make a relationship happy, you gotta ask the woman what's missing, and if you want to make a woman happy, you gotta ask her how, and don't we just have a lot to say on the subject, once you get us started? All of it pearls, pure pearls.

I know you all grew up hearing the saying "If the mama ain't happy, no one's happy." I also know that if you are still married or still with your boyfriend (and if you are not totally numb), then you are with a man who, to at least some degree, knows you are the center of his universe and encourages you to have your way with him. I know that if you have dumped your guy, it is because he thought *he* was the center of his universe. There is nothing more boring than a man who believes he is operating himself. Case in point: Donald Trump. Women do not leave men who give them everything they want. We are greedy, not crazy. We leave men who are self-absorbed, who don't pay attention to us, who think that what they want is far more important than what we want.

Training a man is not a solo activity. It is far easier and far less dangerous with a good girlfriend by your side. That is why Mama is here. So, as I say every chance I get, "Have no fear, Mama Gena is here!" Mama's gonna train you to have your way with men. For their benefit as well as yours. Come on, gals, it's just an experiment.

This book is my heartfelt, ecstatic effort to open new doors for you, dear Sisters, and guide you toward getting everything you want, desire, and deserve from your relationships. I want you to believe that the potential exists for actual friendship, passion, and union between men and women. That is the kind of relationship I am privileged to have with my husband, Bruce.

But creating a great relationship is learned behavior. We live in a world where people understand how to make a living. We spend years at school studying how to do that, and most people who want to can get jobs and maintain them. Au contraire in the world of relationships. I have seen very successful people in marriages they hate. I have seen the quiet desperation of women who find themselves capable of creating fabulous careers for themselves and incapable of creating intimacy with a partner. I have seen men helplessly trying to make their wives or girlfriends happy. I have seen couples who split up not because they couldn't make a go of it, but because they didn't know how to make things get better. I have seen anger replace love. To tell you the truth, I have seen very little love. More like cold war. Or games of what he owes her or she owes him. What I do not see is a lot of fantastic, juicy fun and friendship.

I started out with that exact degree of ignorance and cluelessness. When I was eighteen years old, I met this guy, Guy, who I thought was going to be my future husband. I loved him instantly, and on first glance. It was winter, and we were walking with some friends in the snow at Dartmouth College. Guy threw himself into a snowbank, just for the fun of it. I thought to myself, I will marry this man and have his children. He was tall, handsome, sweet, and so different from me. He went to prep school, I went to public school. He threw himself birthday parties and was on the wrestling team. I was a theater major and my friends and I were all tortured.

From the beginning, I totally and completely went out and "got" this Guy. He was dating another woman, so I lurked until it was time to make my move. On his birthday, I took a bus to his town, went to the pizza shop, and sent him an olive pizza, because I remembered a story I had heard about him eating olive pizza with his best friend: they left the open box on the windowsill, and the next morning the leftover pizza was gone. They had a joke that the Olive Pizza God ate it. I signed the humorous poem I wrote him, the "Olive Pizza God," leaving just enough clues in the note to reveal my true identity. It was not until two days later that he called me to thank me, but when he did, he invited me out to Chinese food at Dartmouth. My plan had worked.

The thing about this was that I was operating totally on instinct. I had read stories my whole life about women who had been swept off their feet by men and had men pursuing them and worshiping them. So here I was, capturing Guy, and thinking the whole time that I was doing it wrong, that it was supposed to be some other way, that my being in charge and making the moves was not how the fairy tales went. Therefore, I reasoned, something had to be wrong with Guy or wrong with me. Or the whole setup was askew. My expectation was that a man would appear and sweep me away to a marvelous life of intimacy, fun, and delicious fabulousness. This is not how it happened for me. Basically, I spotted *him,* I picked *him,* then I clubbed *him* over the head and dragged *him* back to my cave, rather than the other way around. I thought there was something wrong with me and the way I constructed and created my relationship. This man was perfectly wonderful, but I thought it was all wrong because I had done all the decision making and the conjuring. We moved to New York because I moved to New York. We moved in together because I decided. I had been taught the Barbie/Disney version of the perfect love story. You know, the one where the prince comes and sweeps us away into our storybook forever-and-ever land. I knew that wasn't happening to me, so I thought I better cut out from this guy, Guy, and make room for the prince. I didn't want to miss my chance. I had no skills to create a great relationship, and of course I blamed him, and myself. I blamed him for being boring, for not being fun, and for not being able to fix it. And I blamed myself for not being able to make it with this perfectly great Guy.

And the interesting thing was, I looked around and thought to myself, I will just find a couple who is having a fabulous time and ask them how to do it. They will tell me. Only, I looked around and I could not find anyone who was doing great in the world of relationships. Most of my girlfriends thought I had it pretty good and wished they were dating Guy. Older couples seemed content with mediocrity or a life of minimal communication, minimal sex, and minimal fun. My conclusion was that the loneliness and the silence that happens between couples who stop communicating was worse than being alone. I went to therapy and that made me feel worse. But I thought it was good to feel worse. So I broke up with Guy, determined to use my therapy to research every last drop of my anguish from which I could rise like a phoenix and be whisked into an ecstatic relationship life.

What happened instead was that I was celibate for about eight years while I examined, in fantastic detail, my problems. (I have since made up for lost time.) I also found out that many of the experts in the psychology of relationships do not have a clue about happiness, especially happiness between a man and a woman. And I had a lust for happiness. I had lust for a man. I had lust for lust. So I appointed myself the Creatrix of Relationship Technologies, a company and research facility for the study and pursuit of pleasure.

And I appointed my fabulous friend and husband, Bruce, as my research assistant and partner. I suppose you noticed that I leapt rather swiftly from my breakup with Guy to my marriage and husband. All those juicy details of how I found him and married him will follow. This is just the introduction. I decided that if we wanted to get a handle on happiness, we had better study pleasure, not problems. And if we wanted to study intimacy, we should keep on having it, rather than looking at the reasons why we shouldn't.

And if we wanted to have great sensual lives, we had to study sensuality. Bruce and I have now been married for thirteen years. We work together and have fun together and have a child together and have great sex together. And we have been experimenting with researching pleasure as a discipline for the creation of a great partnership between a man and a woman. So far, it is so good.

And these are the doors I want to open up for you, dear Sisters, as a viable alternative to compromise, mediocrity, loneliness, and hopelessness in the man/woman game. We are going to examine how you can get everything you want from a man and have him be exquisitely happy giving it to you. I want you to have the sex you want, the love you want, and the intimacy you want. And all it takes is practice. What I mean by practice is, you have to learn to drop the habits that you currently have which may not be serving you in favor of methods of operating that bring you closer to your goals. This takes effort.

When a prima ballerina shoots across the stage like a weightless wisp of gracefulness, we all clap and say, "My, what a natural!" But there is nothing natural about it. That diva worked her ass off to become so gorgeous and ethereal. You are going to have to work your ass off to create new pathways by which you can achieve the intimacy, fun, pleasure, and happiness you want with men. Training a man is about telling the truth to men, nicely. It's about handling your anger and not spewing it all over him because he has not read your mind. It's about exposing your desires. It's about asking for what you want and being friendly in your communications. It's about taking responsibility for your pleasure. It's about including him in your deepest dreams and desires. It's about using him for your pleasure and remembering he lives to serve you and make you happy. Training a man is about reminding yourself that you are now, and forever, the superior being, and your happiness is the goal of the relationship. Otherwise, the relationship will fail. You do not have to change in any way. You can be exactly and totally yourself, and still have your way. In fact, that is the only way to have your way.

This book will give you lessons and homework. You will do as much or as little as you want. Bear in mind that this is just an experiment, an experiment in happiness and pleasure between men and women. You will be trying something new, which can feel uncomfortable at first. On the other hand, it's not like the old methods of creating relationships are so successful. We have each had our share of loss in that world. My goal is to create a new outlook that will in turn offer you an opportunity to create the relationship life that you have always wanted. And for each of you, the ideal relationship will be different. Some of you will save a marriage, create a marriage, or break up your marriage. Some of you will find one special someone. Some of you will get a different piece of ass every night of the week. Some of you will do a little of this and a little of that. As long as you are enjoying the scenery, Mama's thrilled to have you along for the ride.

Chapter 1

Taking Control of the Wheel

Give a man a free hand and he'll put it all over you.
Mae West

Why, oh why, oh why, Mama, do *we* have to train? Why don't they just train themselves? Why do we have to do all the work? Why don't they come "done," like takeout? Don't I have enough to do, really? Shouldn't *he* be taking care of *me*? Who ever heard of training the prince? How could it possibly be fun to be carried off on his white charger if I had to teach him how to ride? This chapter will show you how to take control and have fun doing it.

Darlings, darlings, worry not. Right now, we are in a relationship pickle. Marinating in vinegar and garlic and thinking it will preserve our appearance and our freshness. Instead, we're just going sour. Enthusiasm, abandon, delight, and outrageous joy are now experienced only on playgrounds or in nursery schools, instead of everywhere as the birthright of every citizen. Men and women come toward each other for reasons very different than fun. We create relationships to prove something (I am attractive enough to have a boyfriend), to fit in socially (I am over thirty, therefore I have to marry and have a family), to create power (I'll get paid more and be taken more seriously at my job if I am married), to become acceptable in our families or social circles (everyone is doing it). How can a gal even get to know a guy when she is so busy using him to prove something, fit in, create power, or become acceptable? I find that instead of looking forward to a life filled with fun and pleasure, most women have a sinking sensation that life is becoming dramatically "less" when they consider a relationship. Sister Goddess Debbie, a housewife and mother, poured tears in class one day at the thought of having sex with the same man for the next fifty years. And she had a relatively happy marriage.

Before I can turn you all into the expert man trainers that you were born to be, I have to get you off that stuff you are on, that belief that you're going to be hit by the lightning bolt of love as you walk down the street. Sometimes I feel like I am the lone straight person in an opium den. The rest of you are all strung out on what you think love is. You are my little crack babies, born addicted to the Hollywood High of love, and I am Mother Hale in my Upper West Side brownstone. Y'all are constantly reaching for that chemical rush to tell you are on the right man track, and, of course, as soon as you get that exhilarating feeling, you are heading for another crash of a lifetime. What's a mother to do? Even explaining this tires me right out. I have to lie down.

M y goal is not to give you something hard to do or to make life more difficult. The purpose of learning how to train a man is exactly the same as that of learning how to ride a horse. If you wait until a perfectly trained horse comes to find you, sweep you onto its back, and take you for the ride of your life, you are going to be waiting for a very long time. Horses are not riders. Part of the deal with man training is that each of us is actually training ourselves. It is a bitch to figure out how to ride without taking a lesson. It is actually deadly dangerous. You could get thrown off and hurt yourself. If you don't take lessons, it will take you a whole lot longer to learn on your own, by trial and error. And you don't get to benefit from the great instruction of those who have studied for lifetimes before you. Mama wants to save you time and injury. If you take lessons, you can become an incredible equestrienne.

A really accomplished rider can jump on the back of almost any horse and take it for a great ride. I am not that kind of rider, but I am that kind of man trainer. I can get a great time out of any guy I meet. I can have him serve me and feel fabulous about doing it. I can hook a guy from across a crowded room and have him eating out of my hand. I know how to tame a wild one, and how to inspire a tame one to be wild. Men love me, and I love them. And I can accomplish all this outrageous flirtation while honoring my husband and our marriage. I want that kind of confidence for you. I want you to feel that you can get any guy you want and take him on whatever ride you are interested in. This is not a big leap, darlings. It is incremental steps, one at a time. You will see progress with each lesson and with each practice round.

And, you see, no one *needs* riding lessons these days. We have taxis and trains and planes and automobiles. The only reason to ride a horse is because it is fun. Because it pleasures you. Because you want to. Your life is not dependent on horseback riding. It brings you joy, therefore, you do it. The goal is your good time, just as it is when training a man.

Does Mama think men are like horses and women are like riders? Yes. And no. Here's the Yes: We, as women, are the superior beings. We have the eyesight, the direction, the desire, and the plan, just like a rider. Men basically serve the desire of women, just like the horse serves the rider. Men can become champions under the careful guidance and appreciation of a woman, just like a brilliant rider can bring out the best in a horse. Isn't it the truth that men are wild, un-kempt, and directionless without a woman? You know how they say that the best men are taken. A guy starts to look like a hero when under the care and feeding of a brilliant horsewoman. That men are not actually like horses is obvious. It's just a metaphor. Men are men. But I tell you, find me a man who has been around great women and paid attention to them, and you have found me a great man. You can train a horse to be a great horse, one that is sensitive and aware and responds brilliantly to instruction; and yet, if you put a lousy rider on his back, you won't get a good ride out of him. And that, darlings, is the reason to train yourself to train. You want to be able to give yourself every advantage to get the most out of every circum-stance you find yourself in, and every horse you find yourself on.

But how can you truly take control of the love in your life if the love itself is intangible? Can you conjure love into existence? During my *long* break from men, and before meeting my gorgeous husband, I was, as usual, studying relationships. I worked at a restaurant (Peggy Doyle's Corner Pub). We served shepherd's pie and had a Chinese manager. Mr. Wong and I got into a heated debate one day. He told me that he considered the way Americans approached love to be very stupid. He said that in this country, people come together when they are boiling, and then they spend their lifetime cooling off. In China, where marriages are arranged, people come together like a cold pot of water, then spend their lives heating up and coming to a boil together. I was so struck by this that Mr. Wong easily won the debate. Everywhere around me, I saw people who were happiest in the first ten minutes of the love affair, and grew more and more unhappy as they remained together. It was almost like they spent the rest of the relationship looking for that initial spark and blaming the other person for its absence.

I began to investigate. Could any relationship be brought to the boiling point? I wanted to experience control over who and how much I loved. I wanted to learn how to take control of my love muscle. I moved uptown to a bigger restaurant, where I worked with almost all men. My first project was to see if I could experience the signs and feelings of love with any guy I picked. I would stand there, talking to some geeky little guy in the kitchen, and I would think about my pussy. I would enjoy the experience of being close to him, of his eyes on mine. I would choose things I liked about him, even if he wasn't my type. I started by picking guys I was attracted to—too easy. Then gay guys—too much fun. Then some serious bachelor types, those dusty, crusty ones who have not been circulating much with women. You know the kind I mean. Whenever a guy has not been in any real relationships with women, he has this look about him, like he's been stored in an attic. I found that if you even take a guy like that and start approving of him and having fun with him and getting him to serve you, he starts looking much better, and the crust goes away. So I even scored with the dusty ones, and I got really turned on to them and loved them. And the cool part was, I loved doing this. I enjoyed every one of my encounters with these guys. I loved talking to them, asking them for things, and I loved the way it made me feel about myself. I was turned on and happy and the whole experience was like a love affair. The guys would help me with my setup, bring me tapes and CDs, let me trade shifts with them. Basically, I was the belle of the restaurant ball.

The pièce de résistance for me was the chef. He was a young, ambitious celebrity-chef type and this was his first big restaurant. The pressure was awesome in every way. He *had* to succeed, his backers were counting on him. He had a wife and six kids. He was so nuts that he spent his whole fourteen-hour shift screaming at people. I saw that his rage was going to ruin his dream, not to mention that it made it so hard to be a waiter. Not only was he completely unapproachable and non-negotiable, but also we never had any idea what the food tasted like. We never knew exactly what the specials were, and Chef would cook nothing to order. Customers had to have their food the way the chef wanted the food to be prepared: rare fish, rare chicken, and rare meat. As you can imagine, many customers were unhappy with this policy, and it made it difficult to be on the wait staff. I understood why such a fancy place had hired me—they were having trouble keeping the waiters. No one could reason with Chef, not the owners, not the managers.

I thought it would be fun to try out my method of having my way with him, for his benefit. I asked if I could speak with him one day. He screamed at me. I apologized for taking up his time and asked if I might ask him another day, because I so appreciated working in his beautiful restaurant. I was feeling my pussy as I spoke to him. He told me to sit down. I told him I wanted to ask his advice about something. He liked that. "Chef, help me out. I am so honored to be working with you on your dream. And I want to do the best I can for you. What would you like me to do when the customer is not open-minded enough to eat rare chicken? How would you like me to handle it? And when they ask me how the specials are, and what's in them, and I haven't tried any of the dishes they are asking about, what would you have me say?" We chatted for a long time, and he finally began to open his thoughts to the possibility that we, as a wait staff, were on his side, and we could all be on the same team. We ended up having a wonderful chat. He moved me so much and I loved him so much for his passion, his fire, and his big, big dream. And I considered it an honor to be a part of his dream. Any time anyone pursues and creates a dream-come-true, it is an honor to be a part of it. After that day, we had these unbelievable food orgies before every shift. He would cook us all the specials, we would taste them and decide which wines might go best with them. Sometimes he would make special dishes just for me, because he loved to see me eat and especially loved to see me eat something I had never tried before, like sea urchin or oysters, and watch me love it because of the way he made it.

I was kind of overwhelmed to see the consequences of my love and experiments in training on this restaurant. I was merely one of a large staff of waiters, but I had taken over the joint. I got all the shifts I wanted, the vacations I wanted. All the guys were a little in love with me, and Chef and I had a great friendship. It was right around this time that I decided that I wanted to get married. And I knew I could do it because I saw that I was in total control of the love in my life. I knew, beyond the shadow of a doubt, that I could melt steel with my love, transform raging beasts into affectionate kittens, and get turned on anywhere, anytime, and with anyone, just because I felt like it. And I was forever changed by this experience, because, for the first time in my life, I realized that that spectacular feeling of turn-on was a consequence of me, and my decision. It had little or nothing to do with the guy. I had the power, the juice, the elixir. I was what you call free—free from the Barbie/Disney poison apple. I had plucked the ice queen's splinter from my own eye and kissed my own princess-self awake to the adventure of love.

I had two friends, Andrew and Mary, whom I had recently met, and they organized parties for people to meet each other. I thought, this is my shot at starting my experiment. Andrew and Mary will introduce me to my husband. Sure enough, Andrew said he knew a guy that he would invite to the next party. His name was Bruce Thomashauer, and he was a hound dog with a heart. I thought to myself, That works. A hound dog is someone who is really interested in women. And a big heart is a great asset. I'll marry him.

Bruce's fate was sealed before we even met. I knew I was going to marry him. And when I met him the following week or so and I saw his big smile and his shiny little shoes and polka-dot socks, I thought, Yes, that'll do just nicely. And we were off to the races. That night, Andrew and Mary asked where I might like to go on my first date with Bruce. I said I would like to have dinner at a really touristy New York restaurant. Bruce invited me to the Rainbow Room. And you know who got us a table, being that it was Christmas week and completely booked up? My pal, Chef. Yeah, it's so true, the love you make is the love you take. My love for Chef was a big ingredient in my first incredible date with my husband. Bruce got to sweep me off my feet because I had set him up so well to do so.

So, for those of you who haven't been swept (or swept yourselves) off your feet, it's time to upgrade to a new relationship model. You know how fax machines seemed so cutting-edge around ten years ago? Now we have practically eliminated them with e-mail. The world of relationships has evolved and progressed similarly, but most people spend their time looking at the outdated model and talking about how it no longer functions, rather than building something chicer, sharper, trimmer, more fun, and more effective. Mama, as usual, is on the cutting edge of the dazzling new world of relationship. We are going to take you down the high-speed highway of your pleasure, your fun, your joy, your sensual unfolding to a fabulous, unprecedented relationship. Remember, it's just an experiment. But under current prevailing circumstances, can you afford not to take the leap?

Women should consider the words "falling in love" to be a red flag. When you fall, you lose your balance, you are out of control, you have had an accident. Sometimes you break something or end up in the hospital. Know what I mean? "Falling" in love? How unpleasant. When you were a little kid and moved from one friend to another, then back again, you never had to "fall in friendship." You just played with different kids. It did not make you question your sanity or divide you from your very soul. What is up with our culture that it makes people so nuts over relationships? Sister Goddess Gwen is holed up in her house right now because she is recovering from some major plastic surgery that she had done. Why? So men would fall in love with her. Sister Goddess Denise was at a card party last night, sobbing hysterically to her friends because she had been on an airplane the week before, met a man she had chemistry with, and never gave him her phone number. Her life is over because she might have missed "the One." Not to mention that she might have missed or messed up other "Ones" her whole life. Sister Goddess Ruth is forty-something and wandering around, passing on so many nice guys because she doesn't have that chemical twinge with any of them. And she still doesn't have that husband and baby she wants so desperately.

We are all so high and we have no idea.

These women, like millions of others, are groomed to put their relationship destiny in the hands of a myth that won't ever deliver on its promise. Believing in the concept of Hollywood-style romantic love is about as effective as thinking that sacrificing a Mayan virgin will make it rain. In both cases, we are going to lose a lot of virgins.

We actually teach ourselves and our children that we are out of control in the area of relationships. We teach girls, through stories like Sleeping Beauty, that the way to get a guy is to go unconscious and let him handle everything. Why don't we just teach them to lie down in traffic? It's much less dangerous. Or how about that Little Mermaid? How healthy is it to teach a girl to leave her element, the sea, and join a man on land, where she will lose her voice and eventually kill herself by turning into ocean foam because she can't live without her love? Cinderella teaches us that other women are our enemies and that the prince, our savior, only likes us for our looks and foot size. This shit is so dangerous. Oh, I am so exhausted from this. I really need a nap.

Whether they realize it or not, women in bad relationships have only themselves to blame. Sister Goddess Lydia from Connecticut washed up on Mama's shore in the middle of still yet another tortured love affair that had her so derailed she had not eaten or slept in a week and she had missed three days of work at her law firm. She was clutching a bottle of antidepressants in one hand and mood equalizers with appetite stimulants in the other. Here was a gorgeous, accomplished, bright Latina woman who looked as though she were a war refugee—thin, unkempt, desperate, and scared, with a hopeless look in her eyes. All because of a *man*. This particular man had been her lover ten years ago in Boston and had married someone else five years ago, after she refused his offer. Since breaking up with her last beau, Lydia has been having an affair with her ex, who has been torturing himself, his wife, and their child with his infidelitous thoughts and desires. Some women, like Lydia, are just so angry at men that they like to pour gasoline on their heads and light themselves on fire just so they can enjoy the look of horror on their loved one's face. Deciding to have an affair with a married man is like playing with matches. And Mama maintains that, as women, we know that before we ever "fall in love" with the "wrong" guy. We could choose a married guy, we could choose a single guy. Lydia made a career of torturing married men—her last lover had been the married brother of the man she was really in love with. She destroyed a whole family with her misbegotten lust.

Some people would look at this story and conclude that Lydia was the helpless victim of many terrible men. The wrong men wanted her. The right men were all taken. Lydia simply was another one of love's victims. Not Mama. Mama says that Lydia is one powerful bad-assed Sister Goddess, blown seriously off course because of a lack of pleasure in her life. When we are malnourished, we lose our table manners. We can get downright immoral when we have not had enough to eat ourselves. And pleasure is the food that sustains our very souls. No one taught us this.

Here's an inspirational tale of how very easy taking control of the love in your life can be, once you have opened the pathway. S.G. Tracy is married to a very successful obstetrician in New Jersey. The man looks at pussies all day and all night. S.G. Tracy frequently went to bed all alone in her empty home in Fort Lee (they have no children), as her husband was often up late delivering someone's baby. She was having a lot less sex than she was interested in having because she always felt like since he was working so hard and up so late, who was she to ask for his attention when he got home? Once she started the class and became a Sister Goddess, Tracy began to see a new possibility—she could simply attack her husband, jump his bones, and go for that great piece of ass she was desiring, simply because she was desiring it. She required no other reason, except that she wanted it. One night, he crawled into bed after a late delivery and she made the move. To her surprise and delight, he responded! They had a hot, sexy makeout session at 3 A.M. and both of them felt magnificent the next day. Tracy was no longer victimized by her husband's career or his hours. He had not been stopping her from getting what she wanted, she just had not been going for it.

I had a great riding teacher once, Donna, who inadvertently helped me with my man training. She watched me ride and realized that while my form was really good, I was leaving the whole experience up to the horse. My thought was that since I was a fairly new rider and the horse had been doing this for years, I could just sit back, hang on, and he would take me where I wanted to go. This is what you might call rider suicide. I would jump over fences by yelling, "Eek!" and hanging on for dear life. It worked about 50 percent of the time. Sometimes I made it, sometimes not. In a million years I never dreamed that my success, or failure, depended on taking responsibility for the outcome.

Depending on the kindness of horses, strangers, or men is a great way to end up somewhere closer to the nuthouse than to your own perfect romance and partnership. And I find that women today behave as though the relationship ball is nowhere near their court. We say all the good ones are taken. That the rest have fear of commitment. That we can't find out where or how to meet the right ones. That we are somehow inadequate, or they are somehow inadequate. Exactly like Mama, sitting on the back of her steed, waiting for him to lead her over the jumps while she was clinging to his mane and praying to the Virgin Mary. My riding teacher, Donna, told me one day that to be a really strong horsewoman, one must have a great sense of internal direction. You might call this intention. Or expectation. She told me to picture collecting the horse and sailing over the jump, and to stick with that internal sense of direction as I rode the horse around the ring. So I pretended I was Donna. I pretended that I was a great rider, and this was my trusty steed. I pretended that we loved to ride together and to jump over fences together. That my horse and I communicated so well, almost reading each other's thoughts, and all my thoughts were about sailing over large, fabulous jumps as we starred together in *National Velvet*. I bet you can guess what happened. I rode like a dream, and so did Horsy. I got on all the right leads and took each fence perfectly, with the exact number of strides. Oh my. So much talent! Who knew? And all it took was an attitude adjustment, a little internal reconditioning. I did not realize how my viewpoint had been holding me back. It was only when I experimented with a new viewpoint that I saw what my potential was, and what Horsy's potential was. We were both fantastically talented.

Let's return to the horse for a minute. Doesn't the horse count? Good horse, bad horse? Horse that wants a rider, horse that doesn't? Is it all about the rider, and not much about the horse?

The horse counts, but really not much. If you are a great rider, you can ride anything. Some will be more fun to ride, so choose them. Some will be easier to train. Choose them, unless you really like a difficult project. In Mama's world, it is all, basically, about the rider. A woman's desires are *the most powerful force on earth*. You can create life, you can ride a horse. You can train any man you want.

The following exercises are designed to flex your man-training muscles. Do as many as you are comfortable with, as often as you like. The best possible way to practice is with your Sister Goddess girlfriends.

Exercise #1: Your Man Training Journal

Buy yourself a blank journal, a bound one, not a ring binder or spiral notebook. (It is important not to be able to rip out pages in a fit of pique.) Begin to record, on a daily basis, any scenarios of communicating with or experiencing a man. We are researchers, oh, sisters mine, and as good researchers, it is important to record what works, and what doesn't. We want to record communication styles, flirtation styles, sensual encounters, negotiations, and so on. Let us educate ourselves about human behavior, and what brings the consequences we desire, and what doesn't. This journal will become your Owner's and Operator's Manual. You will have all the evidence you require to have your way with your men. What Mama wants to do with you is to create a historic document of your accomplishments, so you can prove your fabulous effectiveness to yourself. Your journal is the harvest of your progress in the man/woman game. You cannot help but get better with these practices.

Exercise #2: Turn It On for a Dork

Find a guy you are not in the least bit attracted to. In a safe circumstance, allow yourself to be turned on, in his presence, just for your own benefit. Just sit near him and then start feeling your pussy. Notice things that you do find attractive about him. Could be his skin color, the sound of his voice, or his hair. Why is Mama putting you through this kind of kooky torture? I want you to understand, through experience, that turn-on or chemistry or attraction, is *your* business, not his business. You are the desire and the object of desire, all rolled into one hot little package. I want you to see how you have your hand on the wheel of your own turn-on and how it is totally and completely up to you. Then, I want you to share this experience with your Sister Goddess girlfriends. And that is the end of the assignment. You do not have to date this man or even be friends with this man. It was just an experience of your power for your research and development.

Exercise #3: Video of the Week

Watch *Starting Over* with Jill Clayburgh, Burt Reynolds, and Candice Bergen. This is a classic. Check out how Jill's self-pleasuring causes her to attract this fabulous guy, and have the wherewithal to train him. Check out Candice's hilarious scenes in the bedroom as she seduces her husband by pretending to feel sexy and he doesn't fall for it, because he has been having such a sweet time with the real deal in Jill. Oh, what a genius film. Love that scene in Bloomingdale's. Brilliant fun.

Exercise #4: The Ten-Day Internal Cleansing Program

Pick a Sister Goddess spring-cleaning buddy, and every single glorious day, take ten minutes each and do spring cleaning on "Men." Mama is going to break this assignment down even further for you. Here are some topics that will stimulate your discharge. Have you ever had a cell phone battery discharge on you? All the juice kind of spews out, like the air from a balloon? That's what we are going for here. We want to discharge your anger from you. Here are suggested topics:

1. Dad, father, stepfather
2. Brother(s), stepbrother(s)

3. Son(s)

4. Current boyfriend or husband

5. Ex-boyfriend(s) or ex-husband(s)

6. God (he's a man)

7. Male boss, coworkers

8. Male friends

9. The One, or The One That Got Away

10. Teachers, cousins, uncles—any other category of man

Use whichever of these categories apply to you. Repeat the ones that you have a lot of charge on. Remember, your job is to rid your body of this destructive material. Anger is not forever, it just may feel that way right now.

Here is a more detailed explanation of the spring-cleaning exercise.

You will want to do this exercise frequently to clean your mental closet of all the dust balls, lint, and collected crap from a lifetime of unfulfilled dreams and desires. When you don't clean out your closet—in other words, rid yourself of all the clothes that no longer fit, the stuff bought on sale that never got worn, the old favorites that are too worn out to be seen in public—there is no room for new goodies. In fact, with an overstuffed closet you may lose your desire to shop because you don't have a vacant spot to put anything new. You might even have lovely things that you have forgotten about. Or things that were once lovely but are now ruined by neglect. This exercise clears your mind of all that yucky stuff so it can be open and receptive to new desires. You can do this exercise alone— to a wall—or with a partner or with a small group of friends. Follow these directions and you'll start your Goddess training with a clean slate on which to note all your newly recognized desires and appetites.

Spring Cleaning Alone

An S.G. sits by herself and does this process aloud. She questions herself and then answers herself. For example:

S.G. asks: What do you have on men? (This question is always the same and is asked in a simple, expressionless way.)

S.G. answers: I wish I had a boyfriend right now.

S.G. asks: What do you have on men?

S.G. answers: I loved it when that guy at the bar last night told me I had a cute butt.

S.G. asks: What do you have on men?

S.G. answers: I was so jealous that the cutest guy at the party asked Mary out last night.

Spring Cleaning with a Partner (The Best Way to Do This Exercise)

First you both should agree to keep what is said in the exercise confidential so that you can be free in revealing your desires. Then sit facing each other, either at a café or in some private place. One S.G. asks the other the same question, over and over for fifteen minutes. The other S.G. answers. Then they switch. For example:

S.G. 1: What do you have on men?

S.G. 2: I feel that I want my boyfriend more than he wants me.

S.G. 1: Thank you. What do you have on men?

S.G. 2: When we were together last night he refused to have sex with me.

S.G. 1: Thank you. What do you have on men?

S.G. 2: I am so mad at my father for canceling his visit to me.

S.G 1: Thank you.

Spring Cleaning with a Group

When three or more Sister Goddesses participate in this exercise, one of the S.G.s agrees to be the monitor. She goes around the room asking each Goddess, "What do you have on men?" At the conclusion of the exercise, another S.G. might return the favor and monitor for her. Do the exercise for at least twenty minutes. You will feel free and fabulously energized when everyone has cleaned her closet.

Sister Goddess Katherine was just so caught up in her ex-boyfriend Carl that she could barely see the guys who were actually circulating around her. She did daily doses of spring cleaning for a month. Then something interesting happened to her:

School and studying and spring cleaning has become my life, and a great way to get over my ex-boyfriend. So Friday, at the urging of a gentleman I have had as a friend (translated platonic) for five years, I went to San Francisco. Who calls on the way but Mr. Ex-boyfriend? I couldn't believe it. Caught a bit off guard, I proceeded to practice my Womanly Arts skills. He immediately went into how lonely he was and how much he has thought of me over the last few weeks and on and on and how sad it was that he was alone and how much passion we shared. Quietly I listened and thought, This is what they mean by "booty call." When he had finished, I realized I was not panicking or feeling traumatized, as I had been in the past. In a very upbeat and happy tone, I told him that I had a plane to catch, so I had to get going.

My friend in San Francisco had dinner ready when I arrived on Friday, made me breakfast with fresh orange juice and croissants every morning, ran a bath for me, took me to museums, shopping, and basically catered to my every whim. Much of the weekend he spent talking about "us" and "we," and I am so surprised by it all. To top it all off, sometime along the way, after taking me sightseeing and out for an incredible lunch, he found time to put a wonderful gift of a heart-shaped locket in one of my shopping bags, which I just found as I was unpacking.

I am shocked, delighted, and thrilled with myself for doing all that spring cleaning!

These new practices will eventually create different outcomes. Let it flow, darlings!

But before you can train your man, you must get yourself ready.

Chapter 2

Enjoying the Ride

A girl can wait for the right man to come along, but
in the meantime that doesn't mean she still can't have
a wonderful time with all the wrong ones.

Cher

What Mama will be offering you is a chance to experience your own raw natural talent as a man trainer, as a woman, as a partner in a relationship. You won't believe how good you are, and how sweet it is! What it will take is an attitude adjustment. You will have to quit holding on to *his* shirttails, closing your eyes, and praying that you arrive somewhere you want to be. You are going to have to pay attention to your desires, enjoy your desires, and hold fast to *your* desires. You are in no shape to train a man if you have not already committed to your fun and your pleasure. When you pay attention to your pleasure, your desires start growing inside and outside of you like hundreds of tiny green shoots. Some of those shoots turn into trees. If you want to swing, you have to have a branch to hang on. You can't really train a man until you know what you want, and you can't really know what you want until you have surrendered to your desires.

So let's just take a moment and remind ourselves of the primary importance of pleasure. It is essential that a woman maintain and expand her own capacity for fun as she enters the world of relationships. If she sees a man as her only source of fun and gratification, the relationship is doomed. When a woman is happy in her own right, she feels strong enough to focus on what she wants and confident enough to ask for it. This is not only the first and most crucial step in man training, it is a touchstone that women must return to repeatedly throughout the training process. When we make the discipline of pleasure central to our lives, we create fabulous, fertile soil in which a relationship can flourish.

Most of us live our lives working hard, obeying the Golden Rule, the Puritan work ethic, the "no pain, no gain" theory of working our butts off. It's almost like we believe that if we work hard enough and suffer enough, someday the long-awaited Pleasure Prefect will blow her whistle and call for recess. We grew up with recess at school. Someone knew we would work better if we had at least one recess in the morning, playtime at lunch, and then gym in the afternoon. There is a lot of sanity to such a schedule. Well, darlings, we no longer get recess unless we blow the whistle ourselves. You have become the Pleasure Prefect. I have seen Sister Goddesses work until their eyes are practically little slits and they haven't eaten in days, and they are flat-out panting for some fun, and still no recess because no one told them they had to blow their own whistle. It's all about popping the tiara on your own head and giving yourself however many recesses you can handle. Sister Goddess Gigi, one of my international S.G.s, created an exercise that has become part of the homework for my classes. She suggested we set aside a moment of each day for decorating the house, buying a little something for ourselves, and generally self-pleasuring. When you begin to make a practice of taking exquisite care of yourself and your environment, you set the stage for a happy, attractive you, and therefore happy, attractive relationships.

Now, Mama, what does recess have to do with owning and operating a man? Well, darlings, most of us were taught that men were supposed to enter our lives, rescue us, save us from ourselves, open worlds of fun and pleasure to us, and awaken us sexually. If you think you need a man to be happy, you'll never be happy. Not even in your dreams. This is what you call a bomb of an expectation, waiting to explode.

Most women were taught that they needed to serve the guy first. They were taught to overlook their desires and to pay close attention to what the man wanted. My married friend Susan is like this. She gave up her graphics design career to have three children and live in what she considers a suburban prison while her husband works in the city all week and comes home on weekends. She created this prison cell for herself by agreeing to quit her job and move away from the city and take on full-time childcare, but her husband Barry pays the price for her unhappiness every day in every way. It would not even cross Susan's mind to ask Barry to share childcare or work less so she could work a few days a week, or to get some baby-sitting help, or whatever it might be that would make her happy. Susan has her wires crossed. She puts her own joy so far on the back burner that it never gets served. Her husband suffers from this oversight, as do her children and friends. Her husband never gets a shot at making her happy because she is so busy serving him, which never leads to anything but resentment. Her daughters watch her compromise and they learn that being a grown-up means not getting what you want and being subservient to men. Her friends suffer because she is always complaining and morose. Rather than being able to share their joy, she is jealous of it.

And Susan is a really cool woman. She just has really poor training habits. She is plugged into an outdated model of the man/woman game that will never lead her to happiness. And Barry is a really cool guy who loves Susan. He just keeps doing what she tells him and can't figure out why it never makes her happy.

And when women have the expectation that their happiness is in their guys' hands, they stop paddling their pleasure canoe and slowly sink to the bottom of the sea, drowning in a world of overwork, fulfilling other people's expectations and desires, and getting more furious by the second that a man has not rescued them.

The man appears, but he can't even see his fair maiden because she has sunk. Or he spies her through the murky water, gallantly heads down to give her a lift, and she is spitting mad that he didn't arrive sooner or with the proper rescue equipment. Or he gets there, equipment in hand, but she is so entrenched in the muck and mire of her obligations and expectations that he is going to need Jacques Cousteau and his entire rescue team to haul this buried treasure up to shore, so he gives up on such an overwhelming project and finds another woman who is paddling a bit closer to the surface. All Mama is asking of you is to paddle your own canoe by pleasuring yourself in every conceivable and inconceivable way. Because if we are having fun we don't need to be rescued. And if we don't need to be rescued, then we can devote our energy to creating a real partnership and friendship with a man.

Pleasure is the key to your deepest intelligence, your deepest integrity, your most profound sense of yourself. If you do not pay attention to what pleasures you, you are a hollow being, waiting for someone to awaken you or kindle your internal fire. You are a puppet dangling on someone else's string, railing at the world for keeping you powerless. If you pay attention to pleasure, you are free. You own your own soul. You can create gratification for yourself wherever you go, whomever you are with. You elevate everyone in your vicinity with your access to joy. You enter every circumstance with something to offer, rather than with something you desperately need. But if you have never experienced it, you may never know it's missing. Certainly your guy will never know.

Sometimes our essential nutrients are easily had, if only we knew what they were. Remember scurvy? When we all were learning about the *Nina,* the *Pinta,* and the *Santa Maria,* we also learned that the sailors on those voyages had a disease that caused their teeth to fall out and their mucous membranes to bleed. Scurvy. As an adjective, scurvy means behaving in ways that are mean or contemptible. I know I would be mean and contemptible if my teeth were falling out and my membranes bleeding. Scurvy is treatable with a little vitamin C. A lime a day keeps the doctor away. Nowadays, scurvy has more or less disappeared. We have educated ourselves to include fruit in our diets.

Women today, women like you and me, have scurvy of the soul. We walk around feeling a gnawing emptiness that we cannot name, cannot identify. We have an almost desperate loneliness that humiliates us, disrupts our sleep, derails us from ourselves. We do all those things that our culture tells us will bring happiness—we serve our husbands, our children, our jobs, our families. We ignore our own pleasure. We sacrifice, we abandon our native enthusiasm, we submit to the will of others. And we feel something must be wrong with us because we're unhappy, and we seem to be the exception rather than the rule. And we grow more private, more humiliated, more isolated with each accumulated negative feeling. Oh, the desperate sadness of it all.

And what no one tells us is that we are simply missing one trace element: pleasure. As a priority. As the structural support system that sustains our lives. Without it, we are nothing. Because we feel we are nothing. Because we treat ourselves like nothing. With it, we operate at full-throttle Sister Goddess power: flush, sassy, bold, powerful, sexy, playful, enthusiastic, and irresistible.

Only pleasure can make you whole. It's the only thing that gives us that sense of having our spot in life, in relationships, in the world. And somewhere deep inside, you know that. You know how on top of your form you feel, let's say, when you have had a great orgasm or gone out dancing or read a stirring piece of literature. Pleasure awakens and ignites your soul. And until you experience all the corners of your body and soul, you never truly live your full power, beauty, and glory. If you had a piano, but only played the middle C, rather than all eighty-eight keys, you would never travel to the ecstatic places that Ravel, Bach, Rimsky-Korsakov, and Mozart could take you. Eighty-eight keys are not a necessity. You could even call music a luxury, I suppose, as we do not require it to survive. Although some nights, some profoundly human nights, the ecstasy of music feels more essential than bread, more thirst-quenching than water or wine. It can speak to and inspire one's actual will to live, one's desire for joy. Perhaps it is a luxury we cannot do without. Just as pleasure is a luxury we cannot do without. Perhaps it is our very reason to be. Perhaps our reason for being is not simply to reproduce and work, but to experience the joy and the wonder of it all. "If music be the food of love, play on," wrote Shakespeare. And the thing is, if you never awaken and ignite all your ignitable parts, you will never feel the pleasure and the privilege that it is to be a woman.

Becoming someone who enjoys life and embraces pleasure is a lifelong occupation, just like learning to play the piano. You can always get better and better. Each morning you can take time to pay attention to your grooming and find ways to pamper yourself. Sister Goddess Fran starts her day by blow-drying her hair and fluffing her pubic hair. Why? It amuses her and makes her feel sexy. Sister Goddess Gayle does not leave her house in the morning without fixing herself a caffe latte for her commute and picking out her favorite CDs to listen to as she boogies on down the highway. Sister

Goddess Hannah is unemployed right now and has a very tight budget, but she does not let that interfere with her pleasure. She puts a flower from her garden behind her ear, she carefully picks an outfit that turns her on, and she grabs a little hot cuddle with her boyfriend before she goes out on her interviews. You can choose something fun to wear whether you have two things in your closet or two hundred things. Sister Goddess Sandra has three kids. When she announces that she is taking fifteen minutes of Sister Goddess time, they know that she is not to be disturbed. She uses this time for a pleasure treat for herself, whether it's relaxing in a tub or giving herself a pedicure. We each have to make inroads in our day for pleasure.

We are not conscious of our potential, or how gorgeous and irresistible we are. We are banging on the same middle C, wondering why we can't play a concerto. We are staring so hard down the White Knight Highway that we never see the beauty and the power of who we are and how privileged our circumstances are. Our eye is so untrained to our own beauty and so aware of our imperfections that we spend lifetimes experiencing our inadequacy rather than our potential. What a big waste of time. If you look west, you're never gonna see the sunrise. And you be bitchin' and moanin' and whinin' that you are missing something. And you are. And all it requires of you is a 180. Your glory has been there all the time. That's why you are so mysteriously lonely and off your spot.

You know, deep inside, that you are missing it, and you deserve to have it. And all I want you to do is a swivel turn.

Swing around and look in a new direction. A loving relationship begins with self-love. Instead of examining, in microscopic detail, what you do not have, try learning about what you have. Instead of criticizing yourself, your body, your beauty, your decisions, try appreciating them. It is what you are made of. I am sure you feel comfortable with all the negativity in your life, as it simply is a given in our culture. I want you to become as comfortable with pleasure as you are with pain. What the hell, it's just the other side of the coin. Heads, you lose; tails, you win. Time to flip.

Let me tell you a little tale. When I was on tour with my first book, I was doing appearances at Bloomingdale's all across the country, promoting a fantastic new fragrance by Giorgio of Beverly Hills. I met incredible, fabulous, beautiful women working at these stores and coming to these events. I was in Miami at an appearance, and one of the professional fragrance saleswomen had brought her fifteen-year-old daughter to the event so she could meet me. This young woman told me that my book was the best book she had ever read and that I was her favorite author. I asked her what part she had liked best. She said it wasn't any one part; rather, since she had read my book, she started to like herself for the first time in her life. And none of the girls in her high school liked themselves, so she was lending them all my book. And then I realized what I was doing. Women infect each other every day with their self-doubt, self-deprecation, self-denial, and self-hate. We have the option to infect each other with our self-love. I was spreading the revolutionary new contagious condition: pleasure. Women, adolescents, and girls all over the country are starting to ignite each other with their self-love. She said that just reading the words written by a woman who loves herself and enjoys being a woman made her love herself and enjoy being a woman.

In Seattle, at another book signing, a grandmother in the audience asked a question about her beloved granddaughter. This girl had been a happy child but was becoming a reclusive, sad, overweight teenager. The grandmother wanted to know how to give her granddaughter self-esteem. I told her the best way to teach someone self-esteem is to possess it yourself. Let her see you loving yourself, being pleasured in your own skin, enjoying your life, and including her in your party. She will learn to dance by seeing you dance. We can teach pleasure to each other by our example. That is the opportunity of pleasure. It turns a girl on to herself. Through pleasure she has the opportunity to realize what a gift to the world she is. The only way to experience the gift of oneself is to experience pleasure. You cannot sit there reflecting on your problems and at the same time experience your glory, beauty, and deliciousness.

Ignoring pleasure can actually be dangerous to your health. Sister Goddess Connie was a thirty-eight-year-old blonde with the black velvet socialite headband, whose family roots went back to the *Mayflower*. While she was a successful television producer, and was very attractive and sexy, she was beginning to feel the press of her age as she wandered into a party filled with twenty-something women. At the party she met Scott, an electrical engineer, who was ten years younger than she was. He was quite the ladies' man.

She took him home with her that night and had a fabulous time in bed with him. They got together a few nights later, and he asked her if he could stop using condoms when they had intercourse, as he wanted to really feel her. Sister Goddess Connie was much more familiar with her desperation than her pleasure. Without her pleasure as a guidepost, she felt insecure, dependent on Scott's approval for her sense of well-being, and more familiar with compromise than investigating what really would pleasure *her*. Without talking to Scott or investigating her feelings, she acquiesced to his desire and gave up the condoms.

This was the kiss of death for her relationship with this man, and potentially the kiss of death for her. There was no chance for this relationship to succeed when Connie did not know whether she was exposing herself to sexually transmitted diseases every time she was intimate with Scott. Her thought was: How romantic, I am giving him my life, therefore he owes me his. He thought: Well, this sure has been fun. I am glad she has been so easygoing, but it's starting to feel strangely heavy now, so maybe I better move on.

Scott started to pull away, and Connie got deeply angry. She felt betrayed and he felt trapped, all because she made the decision to ignore her pleasure and do things Scott's way. If she had stopped to *feel* what she really and truly wanted, and what felt pleasurable to *her,* the relationship would have had a different outcome. Pleasure is not about abandoning your senses—it is about deeply experiencing the innate integrity of your senses and the responsibility of your beauty. If Connie had stopped to think of her feelings, she would have recognized that she was putting her life in the hands of someone else, whom she barely knew, rather than insuring her own safety and comfort. If you get in the passenger seat with a drunk driver, it is not their fault when you are injured in the inevitable accident. You are the idiot who agreed to the ride.

Connie could have declined Scott's suggestion, and their sex life would actually have been a lot more fun. Connie felt less in bed because, in the back of her mind somewhere, she was always wondering if Scott was healthy or not, wondering if he had other girlfriends on the side that he wasn't using protection with, and wondering if she was opening herself up to being hurt. Which, of course, she was. If she had insisted on protection, Connie would have felt more, in and out of bed with Scott, and would have been more herself. Scott was not trying to hurt Connie or take advantage of her. He was just being a guy. In fact, it was nice of him to even ask about the protection issue. He didn't insist, he asked. It was Connie who agreed to allow him to victimize her.

All Mama wants is for you to know and experience all of who you are, and what your potential power is. If you understand that you are the music maker, you will never feel that music is only possible in your life if you have a man. Desperation and neediness are vanquished when each of us learns and loves our instrument. You can become better and better at playing your instrument over the course of a lifetime. Let's, each of us, give ourselves a chance to do that.

Understand that your path to self-love is linked irrevocably to your sensuality. After all, pleasure is an emotion, but it's also a physical sensation. I want you to be able to ignite every single one of your nerve endings. It is up to you to learn all eighty-eight keys of your piano. Whether you choose to bang out a concerto or not, I want you to know you can. I want you to know the thrill of the trill of your exquisite high notes, the deep, earthen reverberations of your low tones, and the multitudinous directions and expressions of everything in between. You deserve to be familiar with the aching exquisiteness and ecstasy of the poetry in your body and soul. For no other reason except that it is your divine right.

You have an organ on your body that is dedicated solely to pleasure. You have a vulva. You have a clitoris. The clitoris has eight thousand nerve endings that exist for one purpose—to pleasure *you*. If you are not dedicating eight thousand of your thoughts, eight thousand of your dreams, eight thousand of your minutes, eight thousand of your desires, eight thousand of your laughs, eight thousand of your creations to pleasure, then you are missing it totally and irrevocably. And what that means is that you will feel that phantom hollow feeling, and you will think that a man will make it go away. You will see some guy and decide, If only you can have him, you will be whole. You will desperately do whatever it takes to keep this man by your side, and your desperation and clinginess will drive him further away. There is not a man alive out there who wants to be saddled with your desperation. Ultimately, he probably wouldn't mind if there was anything he could actually *do* about it. But no guy can make you whole.

There are two books I would recommend to you: *Extended Massive Orgasm* and *The Illustrated Guide to Extended Massive Orgasm* by Drs. Vera and Steve Bodansky. This couple knows more about female orgasm and sensuality than any two people on earth. I consider them Living National Treasures. They taught Mama how to come. And I came, I saw, and I conquered. I was a force to be reckoned with before I met them, but I was just a puff of smoke compared to how much roaring fun I have been having since they trained me, how great my marriage is, and how wonderfully "on my spot" I am in my life. I bring them to New York City twice a year to give classes and expand the sensual education of my Sister Goddesses.

You should see my icon, Vera, in action. She can spin gold out of any man. Everywhere we go, men want to serve her, take care of her, or just be in her presence. She can turn the crankiest man into her most devoted puppy. Why? She adores herself, she comes like a bandit, and she is therefore free to enjoy men. That is why my Sister Goddesses are the most datable women in the world, and the women who have the hottest relationships and the best sex lives of all the women in the world. They are women who devote themselves to their own pleasure. And pleasure makes a woman friendly, free, and generous. And there is no way to be generous if you have not gotten yours. And no one is going to give you yours but you. And right there, my precious readers, is the whole man/ woman game in a nutshell—you are in control of your direction when you are overflowing with pleasure. "But what if the man is an asshole?" you screech. "What if he is a loser?" you moan. Fine. Stay far away. Mama does not want you to party in waters that are unfriendly. But I will tell you this: Every man has the potential to be an asshole, just as every man has the potential to be a king. And you have your hands on the control panel.

So, yes, I am suggesting you take all that is yours in the world of pleasure, all that is yours in the world of sensuality, all that is yours, period. You don't need a man to begin this journey; you don't need a specific man to be on this journey. Increasing pleasure in your life requires discipline between you and you. It's the primary goal of my introductory course, "Mama Gena's School of Womanly Arts." We start every session with bragging. It trains women to share what's good in our lives, as opposed to sharing the negative or the disappointments, as is our usual custom. Complaining is currently our national pastime. Take a little informal survey today. Ask five women the question "How are you?" or "What's new?" and see how many of them are able to answer you without a complaint. We have an unspoken agreement to bond with each other in the negative. It's going to be up to you, the Queen of the Sister Goddess community, to change the tide and go on tone patrol. We can hear it in each other far more clearly than we can hear it in ourselves. Between the class sessions, the Sister Goddesses brag to each other over e-mail. We all have to work this new musculature. Improving any muscle requires a lot of rehearsal. What happens to a Sister Goddess once she begins to brag, instead of gripe, is that her pleasure begins to expand very rapidly. The members of the group inspire each other with enjoyment, happiness, and delight.

I receive a load of interesting e-mails each week from my current class of Sister Goddesses. I call their revelations the I-don't-need-a-man insight. It usually happens at around week four in the class. By this time, the S.G.s have all been enjoying each other, bragging to each other, e-mailing each other, and pleasuring themselves in every imaginable way. They find that they are creating an enormous amount of happiness for themselves. S.G. Lucinda e-mailed today to say that a friend of hers wrote her the following e-mail after accusing her of having a secret boyfriend on the side:

> Hi Lucinda,
>
> I apologize if I embarrassed you earlier in the cafeteria, but I had to acknowledge how absolutely BEAUTIFUL you look today!
>
> It is a beauty that radiates from the inside out. No makeup or creams, lotions, or potions could give you the kind of glow you have right now. It is obvious that you are doing work on yourself. Your glow is the result of what is know as an "inside job."
>
> Brava!
>
> Keep on taking loving care of you. It shows very wonderfully!
>
> *Have a good afternoon!*

And her classmate Sister Goddess Victoria e-mailed to say that since she had such a great group of Sister Goddess friends, an intellectually challenging job, a dog, and a newly discovered sensual unfolding, "What the hell do I need a man for? Ha ha ha." And that is exactly the point. No woman "needs" a man. We may desire a man, but need implies a lack or deficit. When a woman makes sure she has no lacks, no deficits, she becomes very attractive, not only to herself but to others. Without the need, you can have a relationship based on friendship, intimacy, and mutual gratification. Here are some exercises that will give you an excuse to become somebody that you enjoy spending time with.

Exercise #5: The Sister Goddess Catherine Deneuve Exercise

Catherine Deneuve began to study and include the discipline of pleasure in her life because she noticed that, by nature, she was not a very happy person. I read about this a year or so ago, when *O* magazine did an article on joy. In her honor, we are going to do one exquisitely pleasurable thing for ourselves each and every day. This could be primping and dressing beautifully or setting an elegant table for a meal or going out to lunch with a friend or taking a hot bath or getting a spa treatment or—Mama's favorite—a few minutes of self-pleasuring. You will begin to understand the seriousness of attending to your pleasure as we expose the differences between men and women. Each of us has our part to play, and the better we play, the more we have our way.

Exercise #6: The Sister Goddess Gigi Homework

Every day, buy yourself something, pleasure yourself, and decorate your home. You can do this in small ways or big ways. Yesterday I drove to East Hampton, bought two cashmere sweaters on sale, had a few pleasurable moments with my Vaseline as I watched an Indian movie, threw out some old clothes from my closet, and switched blankets on my bed. Those things made what could have been a hard day (it was the last beach day of the season, and there was packing and a three-hour drive ahead) into a pleasurable day.

Exercise #7: The Sexy E-Brag List

Gather a friend or two or three to exchange e-mails with you every day. Make sure that these e-brags contain no complaints, only brags about the wonderful things in each of your lives. Make sure that you can share your sweet, sexy side with each other. You can report on delicious stolen kisses or revolutionary acts of self-pleasuring between diaper changes or the new fun discoveries of the joys of being a woman.

Chapter 3

What's Under His Hood

A man will always move toward that thing that makes
him perform the best.

Dr. Victor Baranco

In this chapter, Mama will take you all on a guided tour of the
inner workings of a man's mind. I've done a great deal of research in this area and have discovered a fundamental truth about
men: *Men want to please women. Men actually live to make women happy.*
Though most men readily acknowledge this, it is a fact that shocks
women. In class last week, Sister Goddess Jennifer said, "Why
would I respect a man who wanted to serve me?" It was such a
poignant question, really. My first response to her, in my head, was,
"How could you respect a man who *didn't* want to serve you?" But
I realized that her level of education about her worth as a woman
was so limited that it would have seemed odd to her for the Master

to serve the Slave. When you think you are subservient, you are. When you think the man is the superior being, he is.

This is the come-to-your-senses chapter. We are taking a little respite, you and I, from our tour of your throne room, your palace, your closet, your gardens. We are going to tour *his* equipment. Which is more like the garage. The tool shed. That kind of thing.

Biology 101

The mind of a man can be understood in terms of basic biology. Women have desire, appetite, or call. Men respond to this desire, appetite, or call. Consider how this plays out in the animal kingdom and the heat cycles of mammals. No male mammal ever initiates an encounter with a female—it is purely based on her "call" or her desire based on the estrus cycle. Women are distinguished from other female mammals in being able to generate "call" or "desire" independent of their heat cycles, but they still act as the initiators, not the males. The males respond to the female. The woman can say what she wants, what the situation calls for. Then the man can deliver. This dynamic plays to both of their strengths and it benefits both parties.

To understand how the laws of call and response play out in the human world, have a look at the way a man stops traffic versus the way a woman stops traffic. A man has to dress in a blue uniform, wear a gun and a billy club, and blow a whistle. Right? Now there's you, the Sister Goddess. All you have to do is walk across the street and feel fabulous about yourself. Wear a white T-shirt without a bra and some shorts if you want to cause accidents. Am I making headway?

Another example: getting a date. If a guy wants a date, he has to figure out what to wear, go to a place that has a lot of women, prepare a good pickup line, make the approach, deal with the rejection, move on to the next target until he finds a landing pad. If he gets her to agree, he then has to plan the date, pick the restaurant, pick her up, sometimes order for both of them, and pay the tab. And it's a fifty-fifty chance that he's had a good time. If a woman wants a date, all she has to do, wherever she is, is pick a guy and look into his eyes, smile, and think about her pussy. He is helplessly drawn into her web, sometimes for eternity.

Let's delve a little deeper into our physiological differences and how they play out in the dynamics of a relationship. Men have an organ on their bodies (the penis) that they are not in charge of. In this sense, you can ask a man to raise his hand and salute you, and he is in charge of raising it and saluting. You can ask him to erect his penis, but he would be unable to comply with the same velocity of response or control. On the other hand, if a hot, naked woman were to enter the room, it would be standing at attention with an "aye, aye, sir!" (Who's in charge of this thing, anyway?) At this point in our studies, it is crucial that women begin to understand how fantastically the deck is stacked in our favor. The guys possess the parts, we possess the control panel. To put it bluntly, you rule.

It is time, time, time, my divine sisters, for you to experience the delicious taste of your power and beauty. I am here to whop you upside the head with a "bippity, boppity, boo" and tell you to get your ass to the ball and have a ball. The business of being a woman is the business of attraction. That is when we have the best time. It has nothing to do with beauty, it has to do with attraction. Look at magazine covers. Sure we would expect to see a woman on the cover of *Vogue* and *Elle,* but on the cover of *Car and Driver* magazine? *Fly Fishing* magazine? And there you have it, a woman lying across a new Pontiac, or wearing those thigh-high boots as she casts her reel. Women attract. Men do not attract, they respond. They respond to the attraction of a woman. Whaddaya mean, Mama? Men are irresistibly drawn into the webs that women weave. Men buy those magazines, they pay money to watch women undress. They work eighteen-hour days to make enough money to buy her a big house. They buy fancy cars to impress her. Every single thing a man does is in order to serve a woman in some way.

Men and women have so much in common. Men and women essentially want the same things: hot, fabulous, inspiring, intimate, sexy, delicious, constantly interesting and evolving relationships that grow closer and more fun and valuable over a lifetime.

We can enjoy what we have in common, and we can enjoy and take advantage of our differences. If we pry apart our assumptions (he didn't call yet, therefore he doesn't want to see me again), we can replace them with substance (he didn't call yet because I neglected to ask him to do that). Most women feel that when men don't give them what they want, it is the guys who are deliberately withholding and being rude. Mostly, they are just being really ignorant. When women understand the motivation behind familiar male behaviors, we can free ourselves from the bonds of self-doubt.

Men Are Not Mind Readers

Another shocking truth about men is that they cannot read minds. Men don't automatically know what we want. This is because we often don't tell them, and then we get angry when our needs go unmet. Let's say a man is working six days a week, double shifts, because he wants to buy his woman nice things. But she is mad at him because what she really wants is some attention and he is too busy to give it to her. His goal is honorable, but his method of making her happy is ineffective. She wants something else.

Recently I got on a train from Philadelphia to New York with Bruce and our daughter, Maggie. The only open seats were a facing foursome at the end of the car, and one of those seats was occupied by a beautiful twenty-something-year-old woman. She was sobbing into her T-shirt. In fact, she was wearing the T-shirt on her head. I liked her immediately. I said, "I bet the last thing on earth you wanted was to be invaded by a family." She said, "It's okay, sit down." Turns out her mom has breast cancer and just had a mastectomy. I gave her some napkins for her tears. A bit later, her boyfriend called on her cell phone. I said to her, you tell him to pick you up at the station and to spend the whole night pampering you. He can make you a bath, make you dinner, that kind of thing. The cell phone connection broke up, and she broke into fresh tears. She explained that her previous tears had been because she had spoken to her boyfriend earlier and found out he had gone into work several hours late that day, which she decided meant that he would not pick her up or spend the night with her. I said, "Did you ask him to pick you up?" She said no. I said, "Look, he just doesn't know what you want. You have to ask him so he can give it to you." She said, "My boyfriend is sensitive and insightful, he *knows* what I need." I said I am sure he is all that and more, but he does not have a clue about the world of women. And you don't *need* anything. "Oh yes I do!" she said. "Need implies lack, or desperation. You have neither. Look at you—you got on the right train, you are traveling on your own and managing quite well through this difficult time. And it would be really nice if your guy was there for you. Just ask him," I said. The boyfriend called back a few minutes later, and she asked him to meet her. He agreed. She was thrilled. And she couldn't believe it was as simple as asking him for exactly what she wanted. Mama just cannot stop herself, even with strangers.

Your guy may be the most brilliant negotiator, the most insightful inventor, the most caring physician, the most detail-oriented researcher, and still he may have no idea about the world of women. He may even be in a profession where he deals with women, such as obstetrics or hairstyling, and still he will have no idea about how to read your mind or predict your thoughts or sense what it will take to make you feel happy or turned on. It is almost as if the world of the feminine is a great unknown land with a fabulous, untranslated language. The first step is to have the inhabitants, the women, learn the language, and the next step is to have the language translated from womanese into manese.

Men will remain unable to read women's minds no matter how obviously dire the circumstances. Sister Goddess Wendy thought that the best way to teach her workaholic lawyer husband, Marc, to pay attention to her was to be always angry at him. She figured he would say *ouch* after a while, and ask her how he could better serve her. This never happened. What happened instead was that she had an Internet affair with a man from a different city who seemed to be everything that Marc was not. He e-mailed her every day, sent flowers, met her clandestinely at hotels. Wendy had not told Marc of the ways in which he could take better care of her or be closer friends with her. He was simply sitting on the sidelines watching Wendy slowly destroy herself with anger and disappointment. A no-win-for-anyone behavior. She would sneak around on Marc with her Internet hero. The Internet hero had two or three Wendys in his world. He was having relationships with several unhappy wives who turned to him for reprieve. So it wasn't even as if this man was the ultimate antidote for all of Wendy's ills. He just was what he was. Wendy was so busy living her double life. The children wondered why Mom was so cuckoo and hysterical all the time, and Marc wondered why she was swinging wildly from anger toward him to oversolicitousness. Marc thought that his wife was having a nervous breakdown or that she was stressed. He never thought there was something missing from his end. He was busy doing all the "right" things, making money, cutting deals, golfing, going on business trips. That's what his father had done before him, and that's what he was doing. It worked for his dad, it worked for him. Marc never even thought that there could be something even better that he could do to create the happiness that he wanted for his wife and family. That's where the woman comes in—all the happiness she craves is within her desires. Wendy wanted more attention from Marc. The interesting thing is that if she could have gotten over her anger and asked directly and in a friendly way for that attention, it would have led to a happier, better, more fun life for Marc, too. He would have the rare and wonderful experience of intimacy with his woman, and that is something that makes a man feel better and more successful than making millions of dollars.

I find that the hugest, grossest, choking tangle of confusion comes about when women make phenomenal assumptions about who men are, what they are thinking, and that the root of every problem is the woman's inadequacy and/or the man's malice. The other night in class, the gorgeous Sister Goddess Caitlin was tearfully saying how she is able to flirt with men but unable to get one to ask her out. She was looking at guys as if they were Oz, the All-Powerful, and she was little lost Dorothy. You simply cannot believe how incredibly clueless a man is. He might be just thrilled that a woman is being nice to him for a few minutes. He might think that no one as gorgeous as Caitlin would ever go for a guy like him. He might be shy. In some form or another, every woman is the initiator in a relationship. We are the hunters, they are the hunted. It's just more fun to have it look the other way round. I suggested to Caitlin that she ask him if he was going to ask her out. It's all smoke and mirrors, darlings, just like the movie. If a guy isn't taking the hint about what you want, leave a larger trail of bread crumbs. Sometimes you have to leave whole loaves of bread on the trail, not just crumbs. What happens to a woman like Caitlin is that she thinks a guy can read her mind, know that she wants to date him, but consciously withhold himself from her. Men are not that complex. They are just clueless. Women are that complex, and they turn his simple ignorance and fumbling into great gales of self-doubt or anger or inadequacy. Remember, you have to kick the horse in the side to get him to trot in the direction you want to go. If you go into self-doubt, you and the horse are going to be standing in that spot for a long long time. After hearing my words of encouragement to Caitlin in class last night, I got this e-mail from Sister Goddess Pammy.

> A note about last night's class: what Mama was saying about men just wanting some guidance is true. Yesterday I had a guy call me, and he wasn't making any headway in our conversation and I said, "What are you doing this Thursday?" and he said "Nothing." So I said, "I want to go to the new Spielberg movie." He seemed so relieved! He said "Okay! I'll look up times and give you a call tomorrow!" All they want is a job, they're so happy when you tell them to "fetch"!

Men Are Not Only Willing, They're Able

Men have an amazing ability to produce for women because they instinctually know that when they act on female desire, they, too, will benefit. Look at Paul and Linda McCartney, one of the great love affairs of the twentieth century. Linda was a photographer who, like thousands of women in her generation, fell in love with Paul. Hundreds of those women, including Linda, became Beatles groupies. She wanted to be married to the hottest, cutest rock star of her generation, have his children, his fame, and the eternity that a songwriter can give to a woman he writes about. Linda followed him all over the world for two years, trying to meet Paul, until she met him at a party in L.A. Paul responded to her desires and ended up falling head over heels in love with her, and they created a life-time of happiness together. He gave her a fabulous family, which they raised on a secluded farm in Scotland. He wrote songs for her, such as "Lovely Linda" and "Maybe I'm Amazed." It was Linda who inspired him to create a solo career after the Beatles broke up. Linda wanted him to work for animal-rights causes and become a vege-tarian. She had the desires, he was the producer of her desires. You could look at it this way: women are the appetite and men are the production. Like the fry cook and the waitress. She pops the orders up on the board, and he cooks them. It is a fabulous combination.

Most men have no idea of just how much they are capable of. It takes a woman to inspire a man to reach his true heights of heroics. Let's just chat for a moment about Ron and Nancy Reagan. Do you think that man could have found his way to the White House with-out Nancy? I don't think so. Before Nancy, he was making *Bedtime for Bonzo* movies and living in Hollywood. Nancy was the one who had power, politics, and fashion in her eyes. She looked at Ronald and saw pure potential. I am certain he never would have made that cross-country leap without her desire behind him. Men can't see their own greatness. They are likely to choose goals they feel they can attain. Real glory comes from attaining a goal you didn't know you could accomplish. Of course he is going to doubt himself, but she will inspire him by her belief in him. Nancy had total and complete faith in Ronald. Consequently, so did we. He was called the Teflon president because of his uncanny ability to bounce back from mistakes and criticism. As a result of Nancy's great belief in him, Ronald had an incredible love affair with her. Whenever Ronald doubted himself, Nancy was right there, saying, "I know you can do it, honey!" If Nancy had ever agreed with his doubt, he never would have overcome it. He would still be in Hollywood making those awful movies. Through Ronald, Nancy gained eternity. She got to influence world politics and world fashion.

Men Stick with What They Know

Women and men are wired differently. Men are linear; women are more random in their thinking. Men excel at immediate problem solving—think of a fireman running into a burning building and rescuing the victims. Women excel at the big picture, at seeing the future, using their intuition and instincts.

This is the magnificent thing, and the frustrating thing, about guys. Guys are so monomaniacal, so linear, that they can just keep going in one direction, or working at one task, for years without requiring much diversity. This is good to understand, because you are not that way. You might go to a great restaurant one night and have the meal of your life, but chances are, you are going to want to try something new the next night. We like to mix it up a bit. Guys have less of an appreciation for change. When they find something they are good at, they want to stick to it. Physiologically, we are so accustomed to change that we naturally roll with it. Guys have much less change to deal with. Think about it: once they make it through adolescence, their bodies stay pretty consistent. After women make it through adolescence, they still go through changes every month. They ovulate, they menstruate, they give birth, they experience menopause. Change, change, change—it's our way of life. It's as if we are the waves, and they are the rocks we crash against.

Your differences can complement each other as long as you account for his style and communicate to him exactly what you want. The other day in class, Sister Goddess Rebecca talked about her latest adventure with her husband. They live in the suburbs of Boston, and she had invited her girlfriend to meet her in Backbay for dinner. It was to be a girls-night-out kind of thing for her friend's birthday. She told her husband, Jim, about her plan. Usually on Thursdays she and Jim had dinner out together. Jim was kind of footloose for the evening. Rebecca had failed to give Jim an occupation. Having nothing better to do, he decided to surprise the two women and join them. As you can imagine, they were somewhat less than thrilled to see him.

See, guys are so linear that even though Rebecca had told him she was having a girls night out, Jim was programmed for Thursday dinner with Rebecca. He was so enthusiastic about his bride that he couldn't imagine anything more wonderful than an evening with her, and he had so little focus on her that he didn't notice that she might prefer to have an evening without him. Certainly, in his world, life didn't get better than a night with Rebecca. Jim couldn't imagine that she wouldn't feel the very same way. If Rebecca had

had more focus on Jim, she would have parked him somewhere. She would have suggested that he take their daughter and son-in-law out to dinner, or gone to be with a friend. Perhaps next time . . .

I know, I know, by now you darlings are all screaming, "It's too much work, Mama! How am I supposed to manage all that I manage in my life, and this man, too! When do I get a break? Why doesn't he have to do all this groundwork for me?" It is the new way of the new world, my darlings. If you want a hot body, you have to go to the gym. If you want a great love affair with a man, you have to give him clean, clear direction. And you have to be the one to design every aspect, otherwise you will find yourself with less than what you want. And just like flower arranging can be pleasurable, arranging your life with a man can be pleasurable. Wanna see how? Sister Goddess Rebecca had two choices here: she could pound her enthusiastic, monomaniacal husband into a pulp and let him fry by joining her and her friend and experiencing their icy silence and hatred for two hours, or she could move to plan B: "Oh, Jim, it is so sweet of you to join us! You are so adorable! I love your enthusiasm for me, and the attention you pay to me. Come over here and let me give you a big kiss. You know what I would love next? I would love it if you left us at the restaurant to have our special gal time together, went home, and set up the bedroom for us. When I get home, I am just going to want to ravish you." Which one would you choose?

It would be so easy to interpret Jim's actions as hostile if you were feeling hostile toward men. You could think he was following you or crashing your fun or suspecting you of infidelity. Oh, darlings, the list of applicable shit is endless. But just as beauty is in the eye of the beholder, shit is in the eye of the beholder. If you want to find out how suspicious, doubtful, hostile, or dissatisfied you are in your relationship to yourself, put a man in your life. They are the litmus paper of our relationship to ourselves and the world. If you hate yourself, you are gonna hate your man. If you love yourself, you are gonna love your man.

The Knee-Jerk No

Despite the fact that men are fundamentally willing and able to act on female desire, they often experience a reflex response that I call "the knee-jerk no." He says no because he does not see how her desire could benefit him. Once she explains it to him or simply beguiles him into changing his direction, the situation ultimately works to his advantage. Men are not generally as supple as women. It's harder for them to change direction. They are not as accustomed to change as we are. We are like a little sports car speeding down the highway. When we see an exit that looks more fun than the one we were heading for, we swerve and speed down the exit ramp into our next adventure. A guy is more like an eighteen-wheeler cruising down the highway. When you ask him to change his direction, he simply cannot turn on a dime and change his direction. He might overturn. Just like the Mack truck driver, he requires plenty of warning to prepare for his turn so he can slow down, move to the right lane, put on his turn signal, and head down the exit ramp. A knee-jerk no is not a reason to stop your desires, it simply must be taken into consideration as you design your direction.

I saw a very cute movie called *My Big Fat Greek Wedding*. It was about Tula, the thirty-year-old daughter of a Greek family, who hated herself, submitted to her family's wishes, and was treated like an old, hopeless spinster. Then she decided to go to college and further her education by doing something she loved. Her mother helped her to talk her father into sending her to school. She needed her mom's help because her father did not believe in higher education for girls. His response, when she asked his permission to attend college, was, "No!" When she tearfully said to her mom, "Dad will never let me go to college, and he is the head of the household." Her mother replied, "A man may be the head, but a woman is the neck. And the neck can turn the head any way it wants to." What a great line! Of course, with her mother's influence, Tula goes to school. While attending school, she begins to enjoy herself, take more care of her appearance, and buy pretty clothes. Tula meets a man she had a crush on when she hated herself and her life a few months before. Since Tula has begun to like herself, she is able to flirt with him, handle his attention to her, date him, and eventually marry him.

The "no" of Tula's father was another very typical male response. Usually a guy's first response to any new idea is no. I was at my brother's house this morning, playing in the pool with his kids. We invited the youngest, the five-year-old boy, to join in on a game of tag. His first response, like a reflex, was no. A second later, he was playing with us. It's almost like the guy just has to get a no or two out of his system before he can summon a yes. And most women don't have the protective cushioning to handle a no. Pleasure gives you the padding to deal with the resistance that will inevitably come your way. The knee-jerk no is actually helpful to a woman. It lets her see if what she wants is genuine appetite or desire or just a passing fancy. If you are willing to let your desire go with the first blast of hot air, then it's probably not a true desire. I use my husband like a meter reader. If he says no to something, and I still feel the desire for it, then I come at him again and I know we are going to have a really good time. When we got engaged, for example, I had this great idea that we should fly out to California and take a course in sensuality. I knew I wanted to find out more about sex, and I thought it was the perfect way to start our marriage. Bruce screamed no. The course was too expensive, he couldn't take the time off work, and his father (who he worked for, at the time) would not give him the time off. At first I was upset. I had been raised to think that when my prince came, he would sweep me away in the direction of my dreams with complete willingness, support, and surrender. This was not happening. So I had to get up off my ass and do a little sweeping.

The first thing I did was have a short long talk with myself and I decided that I really wanted us to take this course because I wanted to make sure our marriage had a strong foundation and we had lots of information on how to be great with each other. Next, I figured that I could wait for Bruce to save the money for the course, or I could pay for it now because I had the cash. I figured that any investment I put into our relationship was ultimately for my benefit, so I might as well go for it. I told Bruce that I would pay for the course and I would talk to his father about giving him the time off. I stopped by to see his father and to ask his permission. His father told me that he never took two weeks off from work and he did not expect that Bruce would, either. I said that I understood that, but I did not want Bruce and me to live *his* life, I wanted us to live our own lives, and this was something I wanted very much. He gave me the time.

I think my father-in-law developed an enormous amount of respect for this woman who came into his son's life and took control. I think he was actually pleased that I was someone who was willing to do whatever it took to guarantee my happiness and to get what I wanted. He liked my pluck and determination. Handling the no of Bruce and the no of his father gave me a way to establish my presence in his family and in relationship to Bruce. We all, including me, got to see what I was made of.

Men's resistance doesn't mean the idea is bad, it just means that it is so much fun that they are trying to catch their breath to keep up with you, or that it is simply out of their field of vision. We did go and take this course, and it was actually a pivotal experience for us. It was after this that we began in earnest our years of investigation and training and research in the area of relationship, intimacy, and sensuality. All this research led to the creation of Mama Gena's School of Womanly Arts and our ongoing love affair with one another. So, you see, the desires of women always, always, always lead to great things. And the barking no of a man is just a little experiment to see if you are willing to back the action of your own desires. Every single one of your desires is worth backing, both for you and your guy.

In order to train, you have to find your voice. Here are some exercises that will begin to give you practice directing the men in your life. Have fun! You were born to do this!

Exercise #1: The Con Edison Truck

Pick a night and go out with a gang of Sister Goddess girlfriends. Make sure you have pleasured yourself and pampered yourself in preparation for your hot night. Then go to a bar, a club, a restaurant, anywhere that you all feel safe and sexy and comfortable. Your job is to invent madcap fun, entertaining, glorious things for the lucky men in your vicinity to do for you, and then ask them. Sister Goddess Veronica, from my last course, went out one night. She was on her way to a club but could not find a cab. A policeman in a van was on a nearby corner. She asked for his help in securing a taxi. When they had both looked for quite a few minutes, she suggested he take her to the club in his police van! He said yes! The other S.G.s in the class were so excited by her outrageously fun use of a policeman and van that they all went out together the next week and instead of taking a taxi, they got some guys driving a Con Edison truck to take them to the restaurant where they were all going. So the exercise is not really "man with van," but rather to think of some fun thing that you want, and then ask a nearby, fun, safe guy to give it to you.

Exercise #2: Video of the Week

Rent the movie *My Big Fat Greek Wedding* and notice how the women in this movie control the men. Also check out how Tula got her guy by pleasuring herself first.

Exercise #3: Communicate in His Language

In this exercise, we are going to have you practice getting out of your head and communicating what you want to the alien. I find that most women crash and burn without ever getting off the landing strip. You know the drill: she meets a guy and they have one date. She has fun on the date and is slitting her wrists twenty-four hours later when he hasn't called to ask her out again. She calls his best friend to find out what her date thought of her and why he hasn't called back. She's slitting her wrists twenty-three hours later because she hasn't heard from the best friend. There is an evil conspiracy in her head and she is the enemy target, but all that actually happened was that the date was called unexpectedly out of town for an assignment and forgot to bring her number, and the best friend just never got around to calling. He just forgot. We expect guys to understand our expectations, our expiration dates, our desperation. I wish they could read our minds. Actually, it would probably terrify them. It's truly better this way.

Practice asking for what you want every day, from different men. All we have to do is remember that men are different from us. Dogs cannot fly. Men cannot know what you want unless you ask for it. Sometimes you have to call them to tell them. Sometimes you even have to call them twice. Sometimes more. Do not twist your panties into a knot. Just go for everything you want with everyone you want, and be prepared to account for the differences between men and women. He will be slow to see the things that are of most profound importance to you. That is really okay. You take that shit way too seriously, anyway. My husband still requires several marching bands and an all-girl chorus to notice my birthday is coming up. That's cool. I just start rehearsing the chorus in March for a June birthday. It's about fun, fun with the differences.

Exercise #4: Handling a Knee-Jerk No

Whenever anyone says no to us, the potential exists for hurt feelings and disappointment. I want to thicken your skin a bit, my darlings. Before you ask anyone, especially a man, for anything, plan your second try in advance of your first. For example, when I ask my husband to change directions for me, I actually expect that he will say no at first. Yesterday I asked him to make some granola and send it to our friends Vera and Steve. Then Maggie's playgroup came over and I asked him to give each of the moms a little bag of it. At first he said no—it just wasn't in his plan. I said, "Please?" and the next thing I knew, he was packing up big bags for each of the women and enthusiastically handing out his homemade granola.

Now that you know some basics about men, we need to find some raw material to work with. Is there a right spot to find a guy? Is there such a thing as a "done" great guy? Is there a great guy inside of every guy?

Chapter 4

Finding a Man

Every woman can be creative, sexy, and happy and can
have a marvelous relationship with a life partner.
Mama Gena

So you've done your research. Being the smart shopper that
you are, you know the difference between the steering wheel
and the brakes, the gearshift, and the gas pedal. Great. You are ready
to hit the highway. Now, as you gaze across the hundreds of models on the dealership lot, how do you even know what to take on a
test-drive? Do you pick a new model or a slightly used one? Do
you get a classic and rebuild? Do you wait for next year's cutting-
edge improvements? Is it about safety? Style? Speed? Is a Japanese
make still better than an American one? Lease or buy? And which
has the best warranty? Basically, how to you find the one?

Many women have a list in their head. It looks like this:

1. Rich
2. Wealthy
3. Well-to-do
4. Has a lot of money
5. Handsome
6. Sense of humor
7. Has a great job and makes a fabulous living
8. Caring, compassionate, warm

The problem with a list is that it encourages you to eliminate some fabulous candidates who don't hit your marks. Sister Goddess Naomi had a list. She was thirty-nine years old, divorced, with no children. She wanted to marry and have a baby. Naomi was a power dater. She had guys crazy about her everywhere she went, and she loved to go out dancing and party and have a wild time. She had been casually dating a gorgeous Italian guy, Matteo, who was ten years younger than she was, and a student here in this country. She didn't think much of him as a partner because of his youth and economic stature. She met another guy, Murray, who was everything on her list. He was wealthy, well traveled, and he adored her, wanted to marry her, and have a baby with her. All the pieces were in place. He was the right age, the right background, and he was making the right offer. Murray looked right, but he didn't feel right. She could feel that something was amiss. Murray loved her, was there for her, but she just didn't have that same sense of fun, of being herself, of laughing in bed, that she had with Matteo. The person who felt right to her was Matteo, but he didn't match the requirements on her list. What's a gal to do? Mama suggested to Naomi that she keep all her balls in play. If all she did was to keep going for her fun with each of these guys, the cream would rise to the top. To zip ahead three years, Naomi is three months pregnant with Matteo's child, and they are planning to marry. She ended up parting from Murray because she just kept having more fun with Matteo. Matteo graduated from school, finally, and now has a great job in finance. So, with an open mind, Naomi followed her intuition, had fun with the candidates, and turned Matteo into the guy on her list, rather than finding a pre-formed man out there who fit every one of her qualifications.

Learn to Change Your Mind

Sometimes finding a man is just a matter of changing your mind. You can simply make the decision to keep a positive outlook and thus avoid the most destructive force in the universe, self-doubt. When I met Bruce, I had run the experiment of self-doubt to its furthest-reaching consequences. In the years prior to meeting him, I had dismantled my acting career, abandoned my friendships with my best girlfriends from college, and ruined my relationship with my family. Everything in my life was at an all-time low. I remember the moment. I was scrubbing the bathroom of my elderly next-door neighbor, who had been my voice teacher. He was very ill, and I had asked two of his other pupils to help me clean and take care of him. It was actually kind of fun to clean with them and to help this infirm man at the same time. I remember sitting on my knees in the bathroom, thinking, Wow, if I can do this and take pleasure in this circumstance, imagine how pleasurable it would be to have my own home, my own family, and my own husband. I surprised myself by even having that thought. I suddenly realized that all my years of being angry and doubting myself had had very real consequences. By doubting my ability to experience happiness, I had made unhappiness a reality. I decided that it was time to leap into a new gear. I didn't know what gear to call it, but I knew it would have to be very different from the one I had been using. I could prove, beyond a shadow of a doubt, that the doubt method was a disaster. I was ready to take the road less traveled by.

As I said, I knew I was going to marry Bruce before I even met him. It was a desire, the desire to have a marriage and family that awakened me from my doubts. The events that hurtled me to my dreams happened so fast, it was almost like a dream. Within a month or so of recognizing my desire, I changed my life by starting to take some classes and meet new people. This was hard for me because I had put my social life and my career on hold for a long time. I was in the service business—taking care of the elderly, teaching kids, and waiting tables. I remember sitting on my couch one evening after my new friends invited me to a party, and thinking, I don't want to go to this party. There. That's final. I won't go. And then a little voice popped up inside my head and said, "Darling, you know what your life will look like if you don't get up off your ass and go. You will be sitting in this studio apartment, eating takeout Chinese food alone for the rest of your life. Experiment.

Go. See what's out there." The vista of eternal dreariness, my own creation, sent a jolt through my being. I practically leapt from the couch and ran careering down the street to the subway, heading toward the party, as though my life depended on it. Which, of course, it did. If I had elected to continue my love affair with my misery, I never would have met Bruce, the love of my life. If I had never met Bruce, I would never have my beautiful daughter, Maggie. Without Maggie, I would have never begun to teach the Mama Gena's School of Womanly Arts. If I never had begun to teach Mama Gena's School of Womanly Arts, Mr. Simon and Mr. Schuster would never have asked me to write my first book. If I hadn't written that book, and had it sell so well, I would not have been invited to write this one. Without this one, you and I would not be having this moment together where I get to hold your hand, gaze deeply into your beautiful eyes, and encourage you to get your ass up off your metaphoric couch. Come, O Sisters mine, summon the courage to hurtle yourselves into your dreams. All that is beautiful about you lives there. I know it takes unbelievable courage. But you can do it. I am here for you, to encourage you, to celebrate you, to fan the flames of your desires. The world longs to hear the bell-like tones that ring when you reach for your dreams. Everyone on this planet will benefit when you give voice to whatever it is you want and allow it to come to its remarkable fruition. Leap, leap, leap for whatever it is you are after. You don't need to know how to get there. You just need to know that you want something, and you are willing to move in the direction of your dreams.

For me, finding a partner was a direct consequence of pursuing pleasure. Without quite being able to put words around my actions, I was going for my fun as I headed off to this party. I wasn't logically pursuing a man, just a feeling. Logic has very little to do with desire. It turns out that, at this party, I met the people who became my friends and introduced me to Bruce a few weeks later. I had the desire, they responded to my desire. That is how female desire works, and it's why you don't have to worry about the how. Your job is to just say yes. I could not have known that I was laying the pathway for my incredible life by simply saying yes to fun, yes to my desire, but that's how wonderful the system is. If you keep reaching for fun, your desires will come running down the street after you.

The very first night that Bruce and I met was a Monday. After the party, Bruce and my gang of new friends bought some bagels and went back to a friend's house for a late-night snack. Bruce bought me a bagel: I was touched. I liked him and his sweet, friendly way. It was also important to me that he was friends with my new friends. It was exactly the right adventure at the right time. Bruce asked me out for Friday night, and I accepted. In the meantime, we talked on the phone on Tuesday and met for lunch on Wednesday. We flirted a lot at lunch, so much so that he put his hand right on my crotch, just for a second, which really turned me on. The next day I invited him over for Chinese food, and we slept together for the first time. So I actually slept with him before our first date. It was all so sexy and fun.

During my whirlwind courtship with Bruce, I was continuing to wage my fun war on several fronts at once. I planned a spa vacation for myself, my first vacation in years. I was leaving for vacation a few days after Christmas, so I was going for more fun, and not depending totally on Bruce for my good time. This is a really key piece for a woman. Most of us live on a starvation-level diet in the fun department, as I had been doing. Not only is this not good for us, it is far too much pressure on the guy. Bruce had an easy time showing me a good time because I was already having fun. I was taking fun classes, meeting new friends, shopping, exploring my sensuality, and packing for a vacation. He got to be some marvelous icing on my delicious cake. It was almost foolproof—I had designed my life to be so much fun that it was almost impossible for men not to be attracted to me.

During this time, I had lots of nice offers from guys. And I noticed I was creating a great playground for myself to enjoy men. The trick would be to keep it going, even after I married Bruce. I decided that, at all costs, I would keep going for the next fun thing, and then the next, and so on. I moved out of my studio apartment into a large town house on the Upper West Side, which I shared with a group of friends, knowing that I would have more fun in the company of other people than I would alone. Now that I had Bruce, I wanted to keep expanding my world, not diminishing it, as I knew was my tendency. I started to do volunteer work with the homeless, I joined a singing group, I worked on a screenplay. I made a deal with myself to say yes to all offers of fun, rather than no, as was my previous custom.

Expanding in the fun department is not easy. Our tendency is to decline offers of fun, not accept them. Each time we say yes to pleasure, it requires an act of great courage. I remember reading an article about Warren Beatty and Annette Bening. Warren, in describing Annette, said she had "a talent for happiness." She made it look like a talent because she practiced so much, but it is a discipline. A hard-won discipline that has tremendous consequences. Annette captured one of the hottest bachelors of the twentieth century with her insistence on happiness. It truly is an irresistible force. So few of us practice it on a regular basis, and it deserves such reverence.

If You Party, He Will Come

When you are shopping for your guy, it is best to keep an open mind. Just begin to have fun, and you won't be able to keep the guys from pounding down your door. Most women begin the adventure of looking for a guy with a there-are-no-good-ones-out-there attitude or an I'll-never-meet-anyone-great viewpoint. These are all self-fulfilling prophecies, as you, being a powerful Sister Goddess, might imagine. It's far better to decide that since you are hankering for a man, there are fabulous men on their way toward you. Entertain yourself with thoughts of how you are on the verge of the greatest adventure with the most wonderful man. Here are some free replacement thoughts for the doubts that are swarming in your head right now:

> "If I party, he will come."
> "I am gorgeous and fabulous and I can get any man I want."
> "I am irresistible."

One night Sister Goddess Ilana, a stunning African-American woman, came to class complaining that she had absolutely no way to meet men. She said, "Look, Mama, I am sixty-five years old. I live on a one-hundred-seventy-acre nature preserve in Oregon. [She was staying with her sister in New York City when I met her.] No one lives anywhere near me, and no one comes to visit. How am I going to meet a man?" I told her that since she had made her decision to find a guy, she would not be able to stop the flow of men that would inevitably find their way to her door. Her job was simply to remain open to the possibility, rather than deciding in advance of the impossibility of her situation. She agreed to keep an open mind. Much to Ilana's surprise, the guy she had hired to fix her roof started to stay late and chat with her, and he was twenty years younger than she was. Being a good student, she started to flirt with him. The next week she went to meet her guidance counselor at school. She had signed up for a master's program at a local college. As she saw an absentminded professor walk toward her, she had the thought: I think I could love this man. Turns out he is a widower, literate and intellectual, and they had a really good time together. Who knows where this will all lead? The important thing is that Ilana allowed herself to be open to possibility, which led to a lot of possibility. By taking control of her thoughts, she found several fabulous men.

Sister Goddess Jennifer was also shopping for a husband. She was thirty-six years old and ready for a guy. She had been a high-powered businesswoman at a top corporation, very successful and well respected in her field. Now she wanted a guy. Bruce and I were running groups called "socials" at the time. We would invite a bunch of people to an evening during which we would lead communication games and serve refreshments. The goal was for people to have a fun way to meet one another. Jennifer had attended these socials and was coaching with us privately. We told her that if she wanted to meet men, she could host some socials and get first pick of all the guys who came to the event. She had a beautiful apartment in the Village. She hesitantly agreed to host the socials for a month or so. After the first night, she complained wildly, "There aren't any cute guys here! They were all dorks. I wouldn't want to go out with any of them." Mama said, "Look, Jennifer, you are going to have make an immediate attitude adjustment. The quickest way to find a great guy is to find the greatness in all the guys you meet. Somehow use these guys that come to your socials for your pleasure. Find a way to make use of them or have them serve you in some way. That's what they are there for."

The next week, one of the guys who showed up was an audio-visual engineer at one of the networks. She had him stay late to help her install her VCR. The next week, she ended up going skiing with another one of the men who had a ski house in Aspen. The week after that, another one of the guys, a contractor, helped her hang some pictures in her apartment. Jennifer was having a much better time, and the guys were starting to look a lot better to her. The next week, the man who eventually became her husband showed up. They have been married for about eight years. See, if you just start to enthusiastically use and enjoy the men who are already around you, even more wonderful ones appear. There is nothing you can do to stop your pussy from conjuring exactly the right man at exactly the right time.

The Myth of "the One"

I see women waiting and waiting and waiting for years for that special prince to come and lead them away from their sad, unhappy lives, into happiness. This is not true of any other species but humans, and it has been present in our culture for only a mere blip of time—the last five thousand years. We can recover from this legend and move on to something more fun. Fortunately for everyone involved, there is no such thing as "the One." There are many "Ones" that we will encounter in our lives. Life is spectacularly generous. She can conjure you some amazing men, and then some more besides. You don't have to feel like you missed your moment if you passed on a really fun guy at a certain point in your life. You don't have to feel like you will never meet your man if you haven't met him yet. Know that when you really want it, it will happen. Who knows? Maybe it wasn't until you read this book, got to this particular page, right now, that you were going to be able to have the ability to create exactly the kind of relationship that you want to have. Maybe it's today that you are going to meet a guy that you have an interest in training. Maybe tomorrow. The important thing to know is, you have the power to conjure any kind of guy you want, and it's going to be up to you to decide exactly how much of a ride you are interested in taking him on. And if you pass on him, there will always be another.

The world is filled with fabulous men. Your relationship destiny is up to you, not fate or predetermination. It's very romantic to think that there is some special person out there, and it's your job to find him. But that myth has actually created much more unhappiness than happiness. Most women meet a perfectly nice guy and pass on him because he doesn't fit the picture in their head or that list of qualifications in their drawer. They keep searching for this mysterious "One" who exists only in their heads. No actual guy can measure up to your fantasy guy. He is a real human being, not the creation of your toxic imagination. Just as your skin will never be as white as snow and the chances of your living in a house with seven dwarfs is impossibly low, a guy will never be a prince. Even a prince is never a prince. Look at Prince Charles. Look at the artist formerly known as Prince. Michael Jackson's son is named Prince. Give it up, gals, it's over. You are free. Free to find any guy you think is interesting, and train him. Train him to know women, to honor women, to love women. Then pass him on or keep him. It is all up to you. It really and truly is your party.

Drink Not of Hollywood Poison

My pal Vera told me an old yarn: If you want to be happy for an hour, fall in love. If you want to be happy for a day, get drunk. If you want to be happy for a lifetime, become a gardener. What does Vera mean by "become a gardener"? Put your head on Mama's shoulder and let me tell you a little tale. Sister Goddess Betty was about thirty-four when she crossed Mama's path. She was deeply poisoned by the Hollywood version of love, and she thought the One was a guy named Alex. He was a hot, sexy, savage biker guy who would blow into town, throw Betty up against the wall, ravish her, and then disappear for a few tortured months. This went on for ten long years. Betty was never happy. She was either ecstatic when being ravished or desperately heartbroken while being dumped. Since she was not groomed for the driver's seat, only the unconscious passenger's seat, she sat quietly by, waiting for Al to do right by her. Now, our gal Betty was no slouch in life. She was a museum curator. She was in charge of acquiring ancient Egyptian artifacts for her museum. It's not as if she was a basket case, except in the area of men. She had been taught to go for her goals in her professional life. Her training, like all of ours, in the man/woman game was another story. If you are taught to wait for that chemical rush, and then the guy appears, and the rush appears, you become a slave to the feeling. You think the rest of the game is up to him, and then you are on a downhill slippery slope. In Betty's case, it was ten years of being ravished and dropped by the same man. You would think she'd come to her senses, but that was how she was taught that love was supposed to feel. She was, as the song says, "hooked on a feelin', high on believin', that you're in love with me." When Sister Goddess Betty entered my class, she fought Mama tooth and nail over this concept. How could she even think about opening her mind and dating other men, in addition to Alex? She knew he was the love of her life. She had actually dated guys in between her breakups and it had never led to anything.

Betty had seen *An Officer and a Gentleman*. She had watched *Pretty Woman* twelve times. She had all the classic Disney films in her video library and knew all the lyrics to "Someday My Prince Will Come." She still had her whole collection of Barbie, Ken, and Skipper dolls with all their original costumes.

What was a mother to do? After Betty graduated from the O&O course, I had her take my "Mama Gena Gives It Up to Men" class. I told her that I wanted her to pick a guy in that class and just learn to be friends with him. I didn't care if they dated or had sex. I just wanted her to see what it was like to become friends with a man. Betty picked Wilson, a car salesman, and they began to date a little. They had a nice time with each other, but each of them was "in love" with someone else. One night, a few months into the friendship, they were hanging out talking and they had an epiphany. They were both supposedly "in love" with other people who were not interested in being with them. Wilson had been crazy for Tara, who was in love with someone else. Betty, of course, had her haunting memories of Alex the biker, who had broken up with her again, about six months ago. Wilson and Betty had spent countless hours together comforting each other about the fact that they did not have the one they each wanted. That night, Betty turned to Wilson and said, "This is so crazy—we are in love with these people that aren't even *here. We are here.* Why don't we learn to love each other?" They wanted to love each other, but the myths they had created consumed them for so long. And you know what happened after this conversation? They found they already kind of did. Slowly, slowly a love affair about friendship unfolded between them. And as I write this page, Betty is in the hospital giving birth to their third child. Betty learned how to garden.

How to Pick a Guy

Women always ask me how to pick a guy to train. My response is, don't work that hard. A Sister Goddess simply trains every guy she can get her hands on. Train your doorman, train your father, train your dry cleaner. You will be in the act of training yourself to train. As you begin to shop for someone to date, keep an open mind. Say yes to any offer that looks halfway pleasurable to you. The best thing you can do is to pick guys who have a lot of enthusiasm. Enthusiasm is everything. You can take that enthusiasm and channel it toward your goals. Enthusiasm is much more important than money. It is more important than education. It is more important than a great job. Remember Sister Goddess Naomi and Matteo? She took that scruffy kid and turned him into her prince by having fun with him, telling him what she wanted, and enjoying everything he gave her. That's how you get a prince—you kiss the enthusiastic frog. You can pick a guy who is enthusiastic about anything. I think that blasé, cool, and cynical are highly overrated. When I first met my husband, he was enthusiastic about golf. He played every chance he got. I took that raw enthusiasm and redirected it toward my own desires. I now have to force this guy to play golf—he has so moved on to greener pastures.

I don't believe that a guy's current salary should influence his candidacy. A woman can inspire a man to become a man of great wealth if she explodes her desires on him. I think a woman can cause a man to make lots of money, if she wishes. A man's current employment, when you meet him, is equally unimportant. Sister Goddess Jacqueline was dating a poet named River. She loved the attention he gave her, and the fun they had. At her gentle urging, he went to dental school, graduated, and is now working in her father's dental practice. He is happy, so is she. River still writes poetry for her. Jacqueline never forced him, she inspired him. Poets respond only to inspiration.

See if you can keep an open mind about what your guy looks like. My friend Lulu was six feet tall and found happiness with a guy named Rubin who is 5'7". She tried to break up with him because she missed wearing her high heels. She had also planned to marry a WASP from a *Mayflower* family, and this guy was short and Jewish. But she liked him. She kept dating other guys, trying to find a guy who was just as much fun, but taller and WASPy. Rubin encouraged her to keep shopping. He knew he was irreplaceable.

I think cuddling up to a résumé has limited value. Bank accounts do not deliver ecstasy. Most well-born people I know are miserable. You want someone who is married to you, not married to his job, his family, or his pocketbook.

Beware of "the One"

You really have to watch out for those guys who "fit" your picture. You know that dog-eared photo in your head of "the One." Those

Regena Thomashauer

"perfect" guys are so much trouble in so many ways. Something kooky happens to a woman when she picks "the right one." She starts thinking that she has to behave "the right way," rather than just being herself. She does things to please him, rather than please herself. She thinks she has to be the Stepford girlfriend or the Stepford fiancée, and then, worst of all possible fates, the Stepford wife. *The Stepford Wives,* for those of you who love horror flicks, is a movie about your worst nightmare, being a dolled-up servile maid/ sex slave whose only job is to serve the husband. Whenever you find yourself behaving "the right way," rather than the way that lights you up, you are on the road to hell. When you pick a guy because he lights you up, you have a much better shot at a good time and a good relationship because you will be being *you,* rather than your clone. Sister Goddess Tina was engaged to Dan, who was exactly the right man, at least on paper. He was in the jewelry business, made almost as much money as her father, and bought her a six-karat diamond engagement ring. Everything looked perfect. They had great tickets for shows and sporting events, and they went on expensive holiday vacations. The only thing that was missing was Tina's happiness. When she became a Sister Goddess, she met Rick, who had graduated my "Mama Gena Gives It Up to Men" class. This guy was twelve years older than she was, recently divorced, and had two teenage sons. But Tina had fun with Rick. They would laugh together and stay up all night talking. Rick paid attention to her and wanted to know everything about her. He was enthusiastic about her happiness. Which guy do you think she chose? With which guy does she have a better shot at happiness?

90

I have developed certain prejudices. Take these with a grain of salt. I have a preference for men who have the genius to prioritize their women above all other goals and ambitions. For example, even though some of my best friends are painters, I would never date one. When a guy like Picasso dedicates his life to painting, women become secondary in importance. I like to be primary. Same with doctors. I have a lot of doctors in my family, and I watch as the beeper goes off and they go flying to the hospital. No thank you. I want to be top bitch. Actors? Models? Singers? Naaaaa. Who wants to share the spotlight with a guy who wears concealer and eyeliner? The hours are much too long for me on Wall Street. What if I want a piece of ass and he has to work a fourteen-hour day? I think the most fun that exists is to create a partnership with a man and create a life together. I like my guy an arm's reach away, like Bruce. I want to be married to a man, not his job. But you will have your own desires. My close friend Sue has a fiancé who lives on the other side of town, and they plan to keep separate domiciles after the wedding. My friend Danielle's husband owns a popular restaurant, so she gets to go out to eat when she wants to see her husband.

When You Find Mr. Right, but He Insists He's Mr. Wrong

In these situations, attitude and encouragement mean everything. Men and women actually want the same things. We want someone to know us and love us for everything we are. It's not as if you want intimacy and he doesn't, or he wants love and you don't. No one declines an offer of love, freely given. Love means that you enjoy the person as he is, and that you are pleasured with him as he is. That means that you enjoy the parts that line up with your viewpoints and enjoy the parts that don't. It's kind of adorable when a man who obviously had fun with you and was deeply caught in your web doesn't call. You probably scared him with fun. We all have such a limited field of what is "right" behavior and what is "wrong" behavior in the man/woman game. When I began to date Bruce, he was "the big no." Everything I wanted, he said no. At the time, I was so certain that I would marry him and I was having so much fun in my life that I found his resistance to be hilarious. He was like a puppy or a little boy who just wanted to be bad to see what I would do. I asked him if he would be my boyfriend. He said no. But he wasn't dating anyone else at the time, so I just laughed and said, "Okay, let's just be buddies." For a while, my nickname for him was Buddy. I knew that I was the best thing that had ever happened to him. When we adore ourselves, we have the space to love someone and enjoy him, no matter how he responds to us. It is very pleasurable to love. It feels awful to disapprove. You can afford a little approval, darlings. You are, after all, the superior being. Shakespeare knew all about this. He wrote one of the best soliloquies about how to have fun with love in *The Taming of the Shrew.* In this scene, Petruchio describes how he will woo the obstinate Kate:

> *I will attend her here,*
> *And woo her with some spirit when she comes.*
> *Say that she rail, why then I'll tell her plain*

She sings as sweetly as a nightingale.
Say that she frown, I'll say she looks as clear
As morning roses newly wash'd with dew.
Say she be mute and will not speak a word,
Then I'll commend her volubility
And say she uttereth piercing eloquence.
If she do bid me pack, I'll give her thanks
As though she bid me stay by her a week.
If she deny to wed, I'll crave the day
When I shall ask the banns, and when be married.

Petruchio was cool because he found Kate so right and approved of her so much that she fell in love with him and approved of him and appreciated him. It just takes one loving, joyful person to create love. But most of us have so many good reasons to stop loving: "I'm a smart woman, he's a foolish choice." He has the "Peter Pan Syndrome." He's "bipolar." He has "fear of intimacy." Thank goddess that self-help books didn't exist in the sixteenth century; if they had, we never would have had Shakespeare.

It's challenging to see the adorability in someone who is resisting you because we are not in the practice of looking for the adorability. We do it with babies and puppies. "Here, sweetie! Come here, baby!" we call encouragingly as they crawl across the floor in the other direction. We assume the babe wants to come when we call, he just doesn't know how, or he's distracted, or he is working his way there, slowly. How much fun would it be if we always assumed the best possible motivations about one another?

Dealing with Doubt

What if you never doubted your babe's intentions to please you and make you happy? What if, instead, you looked at everything he did as a step in the direction of gratifying you? Both men and women have doubts. We just doubt different things. We doubt our ability to attract; they doubt their ability to produce. If you want to play the man/woman game at its optimum potential, don't cross wires into each other's doubt. Don't doubt his production, and don't have him doubt your attractiveness. If you say, "My boyfriend will never make decent money," guess what, your prediction will come true. If you say, "My boyfriend will make huge amounts of cash and give me everything I want," your prediction will be correct.

Sister Goddess Cynthia has been engaged to her boyfriend, Barry, for a long six months. He can't afford to buy her an engagement ring yet. But this doesn't stop her. She has brought him to the jewelry store, picked out the stone, the setting, and they have the ring on hold. They go to visit it every once in a while, and they are both so happy about it. She never, never, never wavers in her belief in him. He is happy that she is happy with the fact that the ring is picked out. He is happy that she feels he can do it. And he will. Her belief in him is strong enough to overcome all the doubts. And when they finally get the ring, it will be of so much value to them because it has become a symbol of their belief in each other.

What You Get Is What You See

Petruchio saw beauty when he saw Kate, and guess what, she became beautiful. I saw a hero, a champion of women, when I saw Bruce, and guess what, he became a hero, a champion of women. It's not as if what we see is what we get. It's much, much better than that. What we get is what *we* see. Choose something wonderful to see, and you will create that and cultivate that in your guy. If you think he is a loser, you are following the directions on the box for the creation of a loser. If you think he is a winner, then he is. It is very simple to understand, and yet challenging to retool oneself to see greatness in others. We are so accustomed to looking for what is bad or wrong or missing from ourselves and from others. We don't even notice, we do it so automatically.

I am actually writing this book as a training manual for a dear friend of mine. I promised I would get her a guy by Christmas. And this is the bit that concerns me the most. She believes she will have to get a personality transplant to begin to approve of herself and approve of the men in her life. It's kind of like the horror of those diets that cut out white flour and sugar—at first you think you won't be able to live if you don't get your sweet/wheat fix, but then you discover you actually enjoy other tastes, and you feel a whole lot better when you stop poisoning yourself. See, if you don't like yourself enough to see princes in little frog suits coming toward you every time you see a guy, there is no way you will be able to bring yourself to kiss one. And my Muse is far more accustomed to playing from her I-am-a-loser-with-men side than her I-turn-frogs-into-princes side. I think sometimes she even forgets she has that side. And she does turn men who are not her boyfriend into stars. So my Muse has the goods. It's time for her to use the goods for her own good.

Here is an inspirational tale. My brother Steve was kind of a semicrazed genius as a child and young adult. He was moody, angry, and obsessed with how things worked. He was always doing experiments on the family pets or cutting open fish or toads to watch their circulatory systems operate. He would dismantle clocks, then attempt—sometimes successfully, sometimes not—to reassemble them. My mother encouraged him, pushed him, shoved him toward medical school, and he chose heart surgery. It was my sister-in-law Annie who really gave him a life. She loved his wild, crazy genius side. She thought his social limitations were adorable and gave him more of an opportunity to love her, because he didn't like to socialize much. She basically took him over and turned him into her hero. She encouraged him to practice surgery in Philadelphia so she could live near her family. She had the four kids she always wanted and she used his talents in fixing things to build tree houses and swing sets for the kids. Annie's vision for Steve made him a hero—a great dad, a great practitioner of the art of surgery, and a warm and loving human being. What you get is what you see.

Release the Choke Hold

You meet a guy. He fits the bill. You decide almost instantly, as I did, that he is the One. The only One. And you must have him or die.

Oh, have I ever been in your shoes, and this is one of the worst spots a Sister Goddess can put herself in. When all your eggs are in someone else's basket, you are totally out of control. That's the moment I suggest implementation of one of my favorite dating policies: defensive dating. Sister Goddess Sandy, age thirty-six, was in search of her second husband. She began to accept as many offers as possible for blind dates, parties, and so on. She actually dated thirty-six men over the course of six months or so. When she met Hal, the man who is now her husband, she liked him right away and felt like he was the one she would marry. He was number 29. Sister Goddess Sandy practiced defensive dating. Even after meeting "the One," she kept shopping. She did not depend on Hal for all of her fun. Number 30 took her to dinner when she was feeling a little blue and made her feel beautiful again. Number 31 was also looking for a girlfriend, and even though they were not a match, she set him up with her friend Sue. Number 32 became a good friend because they worked in the same field and could ask each other for advice. The idea of defensive dating is to give you practice at using men for your pleasure and becoming friends with men. The object is not for you to have a lot of sex, unless you want to have a lot of sex. The object is for you to feel your power as a woman more strongly than your doubt. Feeling a man succumb to your beauty and your charm can make you feel gorgeous and powerful. You don't have to restrict yourself to getting that sensation from only one man.

The man/woman game is the most intense, wild, costly game on this earth. It feels as if you risk everything and expose everything to create partnership with a man. Not every Sister Goddess is in the market for this experience. Let's face it, men are a *huge* responsibility. To throw another metaphor into the mix, they're just like puppies, really. You see an adorable, fluffy sweetie walking down the street on a snazzy leash with a matching collar, leaping up to play with you as though you were the most glorious thing on earth, and you think to yourself, Oh, I *must* have a puppy! What joy! What merriment will be mine! . . . Or would it? Do you want to walk this thing? Train this thing? Decline dinners and weekends away because you have to feed it? Yes, yes, yes, darlings, I know there are rewards. I myself have a doggie *and* a husband. But you must be prepared in order to create a successful marriage of beauty and beast. Practice, my darlings, practice. If it's too much responsibility, you can always return him. Just be sure to leave him better than you found him.

Exercise #1: Write a Little Fairy Tale

Write down the fairy tale of love that you were raised with. Which kind of princess were you supposed to be, and what kind of princely rescue was supposed to happen? Really do it up with dragons, if you want them, illustrations of you in your ballgown, and of course, the happily-ever-after kiss. Let's get that story out on the table. Read it out loud to one of your Sister Goddess gal pals. Get a little perspective on the unrealistic expectations you are counting on some guy to fulfill.

Exercise #2: A Man-Training Brag a Day Keeps the Crankiness Away

With your group of Sister Goddesses, send around a brag every day about how you have trained your man. This is different from your sexy pleasure brag because it is about training the men in your world. Keep up the pleasuring brags, too! A training brag could be as simple as you saying thank you to your husband for walking the dog or taking out the garbage. It could also be more involved, like the following brag from Sister Goddess Caren:

> Ladies,
>
> I want to brag about an exceedingly fun girls' night out on Friday. Sister Goddesses Jennifer, Louise, and I (Giselle, we've got to get you a fake I.D.!) started off at Hogs & Heifers with these great guys we met on Wednesday night (another fun g.n.o.). We all three quickly became the belles of the ball, monopolizing the bar-dancing (the bartender wanted me to work there!). One guy who was all into me got into a little ego match with our guys. I met a gorgeous hot girl and numbers were exchanged (we danced on the bar together and there wasn't a dry seat in the house), and a pro football player was stalking me, too. When we left Hogs, we all climbed into a waiting stretch limo (?!) and went to Pangaea, where I danced with every

cute guy in the place and was followed around by international playboy puppy dogs. So cute. In true Sister Goddessly fashion, I pretty much checked out every man in the place and decided, at 4:30 A.M., to go home with one of our hosts, George. I proceeded to train him to give me great pleasure. It was so much fun to have it how I wanted it, show him how to bring a girl up, down, what kind of strokes are most delicious, and then so generously leave him 100 percent better than I found him. I did only what I wanted, and he was falling all over himself with happiness that a hot woman would allow him to win with her like that. At 5:30 I took a shower and cruised to my booking at the *Early Show*, where I modeled very cute ski wear and hung out with the stars. Finally I was chauffeured back to the loft where I fell asleep . . . *ahh*. So who's next, I wonder . . .

Love,
Caren

Bragging about yourself and how great you are doing makes you even greater. Doing this every day not only inspires you, it inspires the women around you.

Exercise #3: Video of the Week

The video of the week is *As Good As It Gets,* with Jack Nicholson and Helen Hunt. Watch how Helen inspires all of her men to bloom and grow by being exquisitely herself and constantly expanding herself in the direction of pleasure. See how her communication skills expand as her pleasure expands. This movie is a joy and a jewel. Jack Nicholson plays such the perfect guy—you will want to hug him and kill him at the same moment. For those of you who missed *Hobson's Choice* and *African Queen,* which were recommended in my last book, review them now. They are so much fun and so wonderfully inspiring.

Exercise #4: Practice Imagining What You Want from All Men

Intend to go for what you want, but don't actually open your mouth to ask for it. If you have a date or if you are about to have some kind of encounter with a guy, picture what you want in your head. An even easier and more fun way to do it is to picture it with a girlfriend. Call her up and tell her that you are about to see this particular guy, then tell her all that you would like to happen. I went on national TV for the first time in April 2001. It was *Late Night with Conan O'Brien.* Before I went on, I had a kooky, marvelously fun idea that I would go on the show and that I would be so good and we would have so much fun, that Conan would ask me back as a guest, and I would become a regular. I told all my closest friends about my fun idea. The thing is, the idea has to live as *fun,* not pressure. It can't be experienced as pressure on you, and it can't be experienced as pressure on the guy; otherwise, it doesn't work. The object here is to simply enjoy having a desire. Relish that. On the very first night, Conan asked me to come back on the air three times. I was actually invited back as a guest four times in one year, which is unheard of on the talk-show circuit. Most stars only get asked on the show once a year. And you know what? I had so much fun with him, I would have been grateful and gratified to have been on the show once. He is such a brilliant, generous gentleman. So practice asking for things, either verbally or nonverbally. Remember to enjoy your desires and to enjoy savoring the thought of your desires. Do at least one of these per day.

Chapter 5

Basic Training, or Driver's Ed

We have been married for sixty-two years. People ask
me, "What's your secret?" The secret is—the man
makes all the big decisions, the woman makes all the
little decisions . . . sixty-two years and so far there
hasn't been a big decision.

Newell N. Nelson Jr.

Guys live to serve us. Your guy is lost without your happiness,
appreciation, and approval. If you feel inadequate or insecure,
your guy will feel like he is failing you. If you disapprove of yourself or do not enjoy yourself in his presence, it is as if someone
turned off the flashlight on a moonless night in the woods. If you
are mad or upset, the person who is going to have to show him the
way to gratify you is you. He will want to make you happy, but he
won't know how. He will ultimately do whatever you ask. Just like
ivy can't read your mind but is responsive to training, so your guy

can't read your mind, but he will follow any direction you open for him. The way to keep him on track of your goals is to expose constantly your desires, your dreams, your wishes, and your directions in his presence. You don't have to lean on him to produce the results, just enjoy the enjoyment of your desires in his presence. You will eventually get everything you want.

At this point in the book, Mama's laid a lot of groundwork for you. You may have your sights set on a particular guy, you may simply have your appetite whetted for a man, or you may have lots of men already in your universe. Whatever stage you are at—with a man or without one—you, my darlings, are ready to train.

The concepts here are really simple, and if you approach it all like it's just an experiment, you are going to do great.

Giving It Up

It sounds counterintuitive, but the first step in gaining control is giving it up. I'm a big fan of giving it up to men. Total surrender, like you do on a dance floor. Notice that if you try to lead, you step on him, he steps on you. Not pretty. I like to toss myself into the arms of my dance partner and take a ride. I like it when a man buys me dinner, assists me into my chair, or opens the door to the car or the restaurant. I like paying my own way, too. It's fun now and then, but the delicacy of feeling when I am escorted is an even greater pleasure for me. I feel so vulnerable and beautiful when I surrender myself to a man.

I want to open the doors of "giving it up" to you. I know how fantastically accomplished you all are. I know you are geniuses of effectiveness, efficiency, and control. I know you could run the world with one hand tied behind your back, and do a much better job than what we've got going on now. I applaud your hard work. I applaud your efforts and the consequences of your efforts. And I don't want you to stop if you don't want to. I just want you to open another door within yourselves, a whole scale of new keys on your keyboard: giving it up to men. There is a design for being swept off your feet. Any woman can do it, and then have the experience of being swept. There is a way to have a man serve you and take care of you and be your devoted companion and lover for your whole life. Call me crazy, but I want every one of you to have the option of this experience. I don't care if you take it, I just want you to know that you can have it if you want to.

This is how much I love men and believe in men. I could walk out my door right now and take any man, as long as he was not addicted to drugs or alcohol, or violent and abusive, and turn him into the love of my life by giving it up to him. I can train any man to become everything he was destined to be, and more. I think the world is full of incredible raw material. I see great guys wherever I go, whatever I do. Diamonds in the rough surround me. I can spot the hero in a man from forty paces. I see their willingness, their interest, their passion, their fantastic production. I am like a Hollywood talent scout for men. I can turn any guy into a star. And you know what? So can you!

I am not suggesting that you should just pick the first guy you run into and train him. Although you could. I am suggesting that once you find a guy, and you approve of him and appreciate everything he does for you and ask him for what you want and relish everything he gives you, you are going to end up with a great relationship. That's giving it up. And I am also suggesting that if you meet a guy who has the finest family and the best job and the cutest butt, but you don't tell him what you want, and nothing he does is quite good enough, and you think he doesn't really appreciate you enough—you are going to end up unhappy and alone. Because you were too pissed to give it up.

None of this is news to you. I just want to lay this out so you know if you are heading in a direction that you want to go. If you are reading this book, you have an interest in men. I want to open the doors of how you can get the most out of one. Our first job is not locating the guy or picking out the right outfit for your first date. We have to look at you and see if you are fertile ground to grow a man. And there is one specific factor that we have to handle before you get Mama's seal of readiness approval. We have to figure out if you are pissed or not. You can't give it up to anyone if you are angry. You may not even know that you are angry, because you have been angry so long.

An Experiment in Giving It Up

When I first started to date Bruce, I had no clue about my anger. In my own fine opinion of myself, any man should be thrilled to get me and should obey my every command. I had zero tolerance for noncompliance. And of course, I had our whole lives worked out. Since I was going to marry him, we would both stop dating other people, and he would call me every day, ask me out every weekend, crave sex with me, and basically be my cabana boy. When I told Bruce he was to stop dating other women so we could be monogamous, his response surprised me. He screamed, "No way!" Not only was he not going to stop dating other people, he was going to insist that I start dating others. I was crushed. Hurt. Surprised. Mad. I called my dear friends and coaches, J.B. and Laura, to complain to them about Bruce. They surprised me by suggesting to me that I get into agreement with Bruce's suggestion. That in fact it might be a very good suggestion. They told me that men are wired to respond to a woman's desire, and it may very well be that my ego wants me to date only Bruce, but my actual desire may be to date others, and Bruce may be responding to that desire. They also told me that agreement is control. The only way to feel like I was in control of the situation would be to agree that Bruce was a separate human being with his own well-constructed view-points that happened to be different from mine. Bruce was not at-tacking me by having a different opinion, he was expressing his own viewpoints. He had not accepted a dictatorship when he went out on a date with me. I was so accustomed to taking charge and calling the shots in my career, and I had such a deeply held opinion of what a relationship "should" look like, and I had been alone for so long that it never crossed my mind to consider that Bruce could be right, too. If I wanted to be in a relationship with a man and have him respect and honor my opinions, I would have to respect and honor his opinions. If I disagreed with Bruce and refused his point of view, I would end up alone with all my fine opinions about how our relationship should be. Hmm, I thought to myself. Hmm, hmm, hmm. There is only one thing to do, I thought. Surrender, Dorothy. Time to experiment, to try something new. Time to give it up to Bruce.

Whew. It wasn't as bad as I feared it would be. It actually felt kind of nice. I liked giving up control. I told Bruce that he was right, that we were not ready to date each other exclusively, and that I wanted him to date other people and I would do the same. I said, "Hey, if it turns out that we find our way back to each other, even after dating others, it will mean that we have something really strong and wonderful going on between us. And I want you to be with me because you find me the most attractive of all the attractive women in the world, not because I am forcing you to be with me." Bruce was so appreciative and so surprised. I don't know if a woman had ever approved of him like that before. And I really enjoyed how sweet and powerful and loving I felt.

Interestingly enough, I did start to date other guys. I found I was very interested in doing this. Seems I had some oats that wanted sowing. Bruce, on the other hand, stopped dating other women completely. It wasn't that I told him to, it was just that I had given him my blessing to do whatever he wanted, and he found that just knowing he was able to do whatever he wanted to do was enough for him. I would come home from my dates and tell him about my adventures. The great thing about Bruce was that he was truly happy that I was happy, and he really wanted me to have all the experiences that I wanted to have. Men really do live to serve us. Bruce knew that if I married him without sowing my wild oats, I would always wonder if I had made the right decision or not. He wanted me to have everything I wanted. I had a much more limited, and limiting, idea of what relationship should look like than he did.

Further Experiments in G.I.U.

I don't think that giving it up will ever be second nature to me. It has always felt like a deliberate new habit that I get better and better at every day that I remain conscious. I practice for the same reason I go to the gym—it makes me look better and feel better about myself. I did not want to be another aging, unhappy woman. I saw too many of them, married and single. I noticed that when I gave it up to myself—meaning, approving of myself, my circumstances, and other people—I was happier. When I gave it up to Bruce, I was happier still.

My next grand plan was to have Bruce move in with me. I was living in the big brownstone in Manhattan with all my friends. I had been living in the city for ten years, and I had no interest in living in the suburbs. Bruce lived in Great Neck, where women got dressed up to go to the supermarket and wore makeup at the gym. Not my native waters. I wanted him to move into Manhattan with me. He said, "Absolutely no way! If I live in Manhattan, my car will get stolen!" Sure enough, the first night he spent the night with me in Manhattan, his car got stolen. His counteroffer was that I could move to the suburbs with him. I did not think I wanted to do that. But I did want to live with him. Once again, it was be angry and alone versus give it up.

I took him up on his offer. The interesting thing was, in retrospect, I see that this was actually the best way to go. Bruce's parents lived very close by. His dad was dying of cancer. That summer, we got to see him often, bake him cakes, and I got to know both his parents a lot better than I would have if we had lived in the city. After about a year, we moved into the city together. It's almost like guys have an ability to sense or read us even more wonderfully than we can read ourselves. If I had not surrendered my viewpoint, I would have pressed Bruce into a circumstance that wouldn't have been as fun as the one he offered. When we feel that we are justifiably angry or that the only relevant opinion is our own, we cut ourselves out of the world of pleasure that our guys want to provide for us.

Everything you do is a move in the game. If you feel good enough about yourself to smile and flirt that day, it is a move forward in the game, even if you don't see your husband or your boyfriend or have a date with a new man. If you sit the day out and are cranky, it's a move backward in your man/woman game, whether or not you see your husband or boyfriend or have a date with a new man. You are that powerful. You have that much of an impact.

Our goal here is to remind you that men are all for *your* pleasure. As with gardening, man training should not be done only because you want to do it. Train because it is a pleasure and a challenge and it brings out sides of you that want to be experienced by you. Don't train because you are expected to or because you want to procreate or because your friends are doing it. You do not need a garden. You do not need a man. Both are luxuries that exist for your enjoyment, should you choose to indulge.

Use Him for Your Pleasure

Another fundamental step is becoming accustomed to using the men in your life to give you pleasure. Could be he gives you a wink or a smile. Could be he opens a door, buys you a drink, helps you on with your coat. Start looking around for any guy in your vicinity and use him for your pleasure. You want to give yourself a chance to practice your techniques on all men, not just the one or ones that you are dating. You can have men fix your car, plug in your VCR, hang your chandelier, raise your allowance, for instance. If you are passing through a grocery store, pause for a moment so the guy standing by the front door opens the door for you. If you are checking in at the airport, allow someone to help with your bags. We want to find safe, comfortable ways for you to practice accepting what you want from men. Take a moment to enjoy each encounter, however small.

Enjoy tossing those lines in the water and seeing who bites. Enjoy flinging seeds on the ground and seeing what sprouts. Feel the pleasurable rush as you flirt. Enjoy the short ones, tall ones, fat ones, thin ones, old ones, young ones. Just like when you were a baby and smiled at everyone who smiled at you and played with you. Enjoy the deliberate internal stretch as you hold back and allow a man to give you the pleasure of opening a door for you. Some of you are going to have no trouble with this assignment. Some of you will need a bit more convincing before you are willing to expand your operating style.

Sister Goddess Frankie had two broken legs after a skiing accident. She had never been so successful or sought-after with men in her whole freestanding life. She was able, for the first time, to really, really allow them to open doors for her, buy her lunch, help her into a cab. And she so deeply appreciated the small, attentive favors! It was during this time that she met the man who eventually became her husband. Even after her legs healed, she remembered the pleasure of asking for what she wanted and the pleasure of being served by men.

As you approach each date or each encounter with a man, look and see if you can be totally selfish about the experience. Are you too tired for an actual date? What if he just met you for a drink around the corner from your house? Would you like him to pack a picnic and take you to the park? Is there a movie you want to see? A concert you want tickets for? If you can find a way to have him advance the pleasure in your life, oh, are you ever on to something fine! You will automatically like a man who is adding to your fun, and you will automatically dislike a man if you feel like you are dating him *his* way.

If he suggests Chinese, which you hate, and you go along with it, you are setting the stage for a terrible night. Even if you have already walked into the Chinese restaurant and ordered, the moment you come to your senses and realize you are hating the experience, get the hell out of there. Have him pay that check and head for the romantic little Italian place that always makes you feel sexy. You will like him more, and he will have a shot with you. After all, when have you allowed a man to buy you two dinners in one night? Pretty hot, huh?

Ask for What You Want

It's marvelous when a woman knows what she wants. A man is so relieved when he can ask and get a straight answer. Sometimes, if a woman is not accustomed to paying attention to her desires, she actually doesn't know what she wants. If that's the case, fret not, my darlings. Just take a little moment. When he asks where he can take you for dinner, tell him you will think about it and call him right back. Then call one of your Sister Goddess girlfriends and see what she has to say. We all know someone who knows all the cool spots in town to see and be seen. Once you have found a place that lights you, call him back and tell him. He will be so happy to have a chance to make you happy.

Sister Goddess Theo was a correspondence Sister Goddess from London. She decided that she wanted to come to New York to meet her graduating class and attend the graduation. She asked her boyfriend, Zack, to plan the trip and come with her. He did so, and they had a wonderful time. She enjoyed herself so much that she wanted to return to New York the following week to take an upper-level weekend course with Zack. She was scared to ask at first because it was such a huge request. When she finally asked him, he was thrilled with the chance to add to her happiness. Zack booked the tickets immediately. He had never had a woman ask for so much, and because of her big request, he got to be a hero, not just with his girlfriend, but with the whole Sister Goddess community. He was so proud. Imagine making thirty women happy at once, by making his girlfriend happy! What a guy.

It is never too late to start asking. Sister Goddess Fran had been married for twenty-seven years and she had always done everything for her husband exactly the way he wanted it. She was not happy, but she never really thought about happiness anymore in her relationship. When she became a Sister Goddess, she fought Mama on this one. She insisted that men have no interest in serving women, that all they want is for women to serve them. I asked her if she had ever tried simply asking a man for something she wanted. Fran said that she had never tried. I asked her to experiment just once and then report back to the class. When she got home that night, Fran practiced exposing a desire. She asked her husband to go upstairs and get her slippers for her. Without hesitation, he obliged. She had a flood of emotion as he brought her the slippers. Imagine, how easy that was. She sat in the chair holding the slippers, tears in her eyes. Imagine how he might have given her what she wanted all these years, if she had only asked. Imagine the love that was lost. But Mama heartily discourages backward-glancing. When you look at the past with your new eyesight, all you can see is loss. When you look at the future, there is worry or fear. All we have is fleeting, sweet, perfect now. Fran is one of the few women on the planet who has opened the door to a new way of loving herself and her husband. She experimented with the new style of partnership, with her desires guiding his production. Even if she never asks him for another thing again, Fran now knows she has a man who is willing to serve her. Most women live their entire lives without knowing and experiencing the best friend that they have in their men. If you don't ask, you will never receive.

Only Say Yes When You Really Mean Yes

When Sister Goddess Jane came to class, she was twenty-nine years old, and she had never ordered what she really, really wanted in a restaurant, on a date with a man. She ordered what she thought he would approve of. Or what she thought he could afford. Or what would make her seem low maintenance, or not leave her with the obligation of payback sex. (Lobster and champagne was high maintenance, payback sex material; pasta and club soda was low maintenance, no obligation.) There was a whole code of operations going on in her head that her date had no idea about, and that had no relationship to her pleasure. Her pleasure was the very last thing she thought about. And she never had a boyfriend who stuck around very long. The guys would drift away from Jane because they never really felt like they made her happy. And guys love to make us happy. They live for it.

After her O&O course with me, Jane went out to dinner with a new guy. She ordered her first lobster. Jane grew up in Maine, and lobster had deep cultural significance for her. She called me from the restaurant to express her great joy and delight in her own bodaciousness. She was thrilled with herself and thrilled with her date. She held him responsible for this wonderful experience. And she had a really, really good time with this man, and he with her. Hey, it was just a hunk of shellfish, a difference of a few dollars on the check, you may say. But it was a whole new world for Jane, and for millions of women who will never even consider giving themselves the luxury of knowing what they want, and then bringing their guy into *their* world of what pleasures *them*.

Guys are going to make all kinds of offers to you. Some will be fun offers, and some will seem horrible or even insulting. Experiment by accepting only the offers that really light you up. And experiment by educating your guy about how he can make you even more pleasurable offers. Remember that a guy is only as good as his previous training, so when he asks you to come over and wash the car with him, know that you can turn him down nicely and suggest that he pick you up after the car is washed and take you for a drive to see the fall foliage.

Tell the Whole Truth

Telling all of your thoughts and observations and desires to a man is a very new experience for women. You will be uncomfortable. He may be uncomfortable. But it is the only way your relationship and your well-being will thrive. You are the only one who can create room in your relationship for *you*. You carve out your space one truth at a time.

Here's a familiar tale. Sister Goddess Violet was the caretaker for her family in Westchester. As the youngest of her three kids entered school, she wanted to have more help from her husband, Gary. She wanted to write, spend more time at the gym, and cut down on her hours at the office. She asked Gary to pitch in with the dinners, the bedtimes, and the housework. Gary refused to cooperate. He had his little routine of working late at his advertising company and coming home to a clean house with dinner on the table. Why fix it if it ain't broke? thought Gary. He had been doing things this way for ten years, and he could not really see why he had to change. Violet grew more and more angry with Gary, more and more distanced, more silent, and finally began a little affair with her daughter's third-grade teacher. It seemed easier to start an affair than to find a way to teach her old dog new tricks. Her anger at her old dog and at herself kept her from carving out a new phase in her relationship with her husband.

I do hope I am giving you a little food for thought. What Mama is suggesting is that you can actually create, in partnership with your man, exactly the right relationship mix for you. Everyone ultimately does this, but first they usually blame their partner for failing them in some crucial way, rather than taking deliberate control of their desires and their intimacy with another human being. When Gary failed to respond instantly to Violet's new desires, she began an affair. She did not say, "I want to have an affair, Gary. Let's work this out so we can both be happy." She did not say, "Your actions are so upsetting to me that I feel you are not interested in being my friend, and I really want you to be my friend in this!" Or, "Gary, it's my way or the highway." Mama's thought is that we can, with courage and communication, have our cake and eat it, too. Violet took the low road, cheating behind her husband's back. You can't educate a man if you won't communicate the truth to him. Mama is suggesting that we each do whatever it takes to live with integrity and full-throttle joy. It requires a lot of courage to live an exquisite life, but anything less simply isn't enough for a Sister Goddess.

Sister Goddess Avery learned her lesson the hard way. When Avery moved in with her boyfriend, who lived in Chicago, she wanted everything to be perfect. She wanted to be a slut in the bedroom and a lady in the living room. Problem was, she lacked a housekeeping gene. She was, and is, revolted by housework. Her boyfriend, Keith, grew up in a house where his mom did all the housecleaning herself for the whole family. In Keith's world, women not only did that sort of thing, but they liked to do that sort of thing. Avery felt deeply inadequate. She loved Keith, but she didn't love cleaning bathrooms or vacuuming floors. She felt Keith wouldn't love her if she didn't love housework. Instead of sitting him down and telling him she really wanted him to hire a maid, she took an extra shift at her nursing job each week and quietly paid for a housekeeper to come in every Thursday to clean the place. At first, Avery thought she was really getting away with it. Clean apartment, no problem. But every time that Keith would notice the clean apartment and say how nice it looked, she would get angry at him for being such an idiot. How could he not notice that she hated housework? How could he expect that she would work full-time, and then come home and clean full-time? What was his contribution? What was he, stupid?

As you can probably imagine, this arrangement couldn't possibly last. Buried treasure becomes a thorn in one's side if it is not brought up to enjoy in the light of day. Avery moved out of Keith's place and back into her own because he wasn't giving her what she wanted. Pissed instead of blissed. After a few months apart and another class with Mama, Avery got back together with Keith. She realized that if she was not going to tell him what she wanted, there was no way they would be able to find happiness. At first it was a little shocking to Keith that a woman would want to do something different from what his mom had done, but once Avery laid it all out for him, he could really understand that his expectation was a bit unrealistic, given their work schedules. He had just never thought about it like that. This time, they split the cost of the maid. And had a few good laughs, besides. Avery told him that it was a bit challenging for her to say what she wanted, and if he could check in with her sometimes, especially when she seemed unusually silent, and ask her, "What's up?" she would really appreciate it.

A relationship is over the moment you stop telling your truth. Exposing your desires to a man takes practice. Women were brought up to be "nice" and serve others and take care of their jobs, families, and men. We weren't taught to serve our own desires. But you gotta look at the evidence. In a world full of women serving men, we have boatloads of unhappiness and conflict between men and women. Time to try a new tack, even if it is simply as an experiment.

Truth Without Anger

Women always think that they can't say the truth to men, that it will offend them or put them off. In fact, it is the most refreshing thing on earth for a man to hear what a woman thinks. I know a really hot lesbian, Sister Goddess Valeria, who takes my classes. Valeria has guys eating out of her hand because she is friendly and truthful with them. She is not trying to lure them or catch them in her web. She is just utterly herself. I have her come to the "Mama Gives It Up to Men" class and tell the guys how to kiss and how to suck pussy. The men love her because she tells them what they really need to know and holds nothing back. So just practice saying your thoughts. If you had a nice time on your date, call him up and tell him. If you want to see him again, suggest that. If you find yourself trying to strong-arm him into asking you out again, confess that that is what you are doing. If you are feeling cranky, say so. Like that. Truth, truth, truth, nothin' but the truth. As if he was a girlfriend.

Here's another example. Sister Goddess Daphne went out on a

date with a guy with hair plugs. Other than the plugs, he was an amazing man. He was sweet, well-read, intelligent, thoughtful, and he really liked Daphne. Daphne had a thought: How could I ever let a guy with hair plugs suck my pussy? If I look down there and see all those plugs, I will either start to laugh or be totally grossed out. Daphne decided that she could not possibly tell this man her feelings about his plugs, because, the thing was, he was president of the Hair Plug Society. Hair plugs were his life. So she just stopped seeing him. After a little truth serum from Mama, Daphne picked up the phone and asked the president to meet her for coffee. She told him that she was doing this experiment of telling the truth to men, and she told him that she really liked him, but she had this weird thought about his hair plugs in bed. The president was so flattered that she had been even thinking about having sex with him. He was thrilled. They actually had a good laugh about it. He offered to wear a baseball cap. They ended up having a great time flirting and laughing and imagining ways around the situation. Daphne noticed that this guy, with his sense of humor and willingness, really turned her on. She actually found that she was having thoughts about wanting that baseball cap you-know-where. If she had kept her original "negative" thoughts to herself, she would never have had this great opening to a potential romance with Mr. President.

They say that the definition of insanity is doing the same thing over and over again and expecting a different outcome. But I know that trying something new feels so very uncomfortable. It is not easy to be a pioneer. Lewis and Clark did not know where the hell they were going as they mapped the Louisiana Purchase. You will feel weird and somewhat lost and quite vulnerable as you expose your desires to a man. That is okay. That's what a trailblazer feels like. If you begin to feel comfortable, watch out, because you are slipping back into what doesn't work—your silence, your compromise, and the absence of desire. Don't go there. That is the world of Pissy, not Pussy. I have not hauled your ass this far to lose you now. Hang on, gals. Every time you expose a desire to a man, you make it easier for some woman somewhere, somehow, to do the same.

Don't Give Up On Something You Want

Sister Goddess Hannah's husband, Mike, got a job in Baltimore, three hours away from the small town outside of Philadelphia where they had been living for the past fifteen years. Hannah arranged to fix up the house in order to sell it. She found a house she loved in Baltimore, and on the very day they were to sign the papers to sell the house in Philadelphia, Mike freaked out. He could not bring himself to sign. He was so upset. Instead of hanging tight to her dream of a new life in a new town, close to her husband's job, Hannah folded. She canceled the sale and stopped the purchase of her dream house. Here it is, six months later, and Hannah is basically a single parent as her husband drives three hours to and from work, leaving her to help with homework, make dinner, clean up, bathe and put four kids to bed each night, all without any help. Sometimes he stays over in Baltimore, leaving her with even more to handle. If she had held out for what she really wanted, despite his kicking and screaming, it would be a much more pleasurable life for both of them.

Saying the truth will make you sweat, then it will set you free. In the beginning of this experiment, it feels almost torturous to expose a desire. And then, if your guy declines, it feels almost unendurable, as if you will crumple up and blow away like an old newspaper. What you have to remember is that you are learning a new skill set. You are unlocking desires that have been in the vault for centuries and appreciating the alien enemy. Think Arabs and Jews here for a minute. Think Muslims and Hindus. It's a centuries-old war, and I am asking you to offer the olive branch.

There is nothing more powerful than exposing a desire, and nothing that will make you feel more vulnerable. When I was first dating Bruce, I didn't like the way he kissed me. He kissed me strongly and with a lot of tongue, the way that his last girlfriend liked it. But I had another way that I liked—very soft, gentle, with a lot of breath and lightly touching lips and cheeks, then slightly open mouth and light tongue, then slowly deeper. I remember the moment when I was exposing my desire to Bruce about the way I wanted to be kissed—I felt like I was going to have a heart attack. I was sweating, felt nauseous, and could barely explain. I felt like he would be insulted or offended, and who was I to think my way was better, and why would he want to kiss me my way? Surprisingly to me, he was cool. He asked me to show him what I meant. I told him to remain still, and I would take him on a tour of my kind of kiss. Sweaty butterflies and all, I slowly kissed him. And I still remember every detail of that kiss. I remember that with the stillness between us, I could really feel him and taste him and enjoy the sensation of his skin on mine, his breath mingling with mine. I grew weak in the knees with the beautiful flood of feeling as he held me in his arms. Bruce swept me off my feet. And he never would have had a shot at kissing me that way unless I exposed my desire to him. The bonus is, he still kisses me exactly like that. Once you tell a guy something you want and he really understands it, it becomes a permanent part of the mainframe and the hard drive. It is inputted forever and will always be there for you.

Approve of This Man

It feels wonderful to approve of and appreciate someone. Allow yourself to enjoy every aspect of having a man in your life. Enjoy his attention to you and contribution to you. Sure, there are some things you may wish to experience a little differently, but you don't have to stop approving of him to have your way. Many women plunge straight from a small disappointment to outrageous hostility and anger. Anger doesn't instruct, doesn't elevate, doesn't inform. If you can stay in friendly rapport with him, you will feel great about yourself and great about your training. I always say that if women were as friendly to their men as they are to their dogs, we would have the basis for magnificent relationships.

Most women have a tendency to think that if they have goals, whatever they get from their guy that doesn't measure up to their goals is wrong or inadequate. We are always in such a rush. When I first met Bruce, I announced to everyone I met that I had just met my future husband. I told my mother, my sister-in-law—well, everyone. They were all so desperate for me to get married, and also so happy for me, that my sister-in-law wanted to throw me an engagement brunch so Bruce could meet the family. I suppose I should mention that this was about a month after I met him. Bruce could feel the noose tightening around his neck, and he rebelled. He refused to go to the party. I was hurt, humiliated, shocked, upset. And I was vastly angry at Bruce. How could *he* put *me* in this terribly embarrassing, humiliating position with my family? Could I ever be seen in public again? How could I ever talk to him, or anyone in my family, ever again? But when I came to my senses, I realized that there was no way that Bruce could feel comfortable with this particular invitation. I was forcing him into something because of my ego—I wanted to prove to my family that I was not the outcast spinster, the only unmarried daughter of my family. I wanted to demonstrate that I was not a failure in relationships. Bruce could feel that this party was an unnecessary ego trip about me and my sense of inadequacy, not a celebration of our friendship and love. Of course he refused to go. And of course I was humiliated. But it was a great lesson for me. Plunged headlong into the belly of my doubts, I had to learn that I was in a *relationship,* not an ego trip. I was forced to decide which was more important to me, maintaining my friendship with Bruce or impressing my family. I chose Bruce. Barely. As an experiment. I wanted to hate him and live in my anger and disappointment, but I decided just to experiment with making a 180 swing around out of my doubts and into surrendering to my guy's point of view. This was a place I had never been before. And you know what? That was the best way to impress my family. I told them that the party was premature, that I had put Bruce in an uncomfortable position, and that we would meet them at some other time. I decided that rather than be angry at him for "disappointing me," I would treat his decision as a gift. Which it was—it was a gift for us to have the opportunity to move toward experiences as a team, not me, Miss Bossy Ass, forcing him to comply to my version of what my familial expectations were.

Thank You Gets You More

There is another part to this training thing. Once you have a man giving you what you want, it is very important to acknowledge what you are receiving. Acknowledgment is just a friendly little "thank you." Or it can simply be a smile. When you acknowledge someone for doing something nice for you, you feel good and they feel good. If you don't acknowledge, you don't get that good feeling. You also won't be able to have more. Acknowledgment is kind of like chewing and swallowing the food that is in your mouth. If someone makes you a lovely dinner, but you don't chew it and swallow it, you won't have any room in your mouth for dessert. Many times, women are so overall—in general, just on principle— angry at men and angry at the world, that they simply do not acknowledge a guy, even when he does something really lovely for them. And the acknowledgment is not for the guy. Men live to serve us. They love to make us happy and will continue to do that, whether or not we ever say "thanks." The acknowledgment is for you. It's so you can relish the experience, so you can feel the impact of your desires, so you can make room inside of you to have more.

Sister Goddess Clara came to Mama Gena's School of Womanly Arts in order to become even more of the woman that she is, and to conjure a great love affair with a man. On Valentine's Day, she was in the mood for romance. She went to a party in Connecticut and met an architect named Gabriel. He lived in the house next door to where the party was being given, and he invited Clara to come see his home. She walked in and felt a chill: "This is the man I am going to marry and we will live here and raise our children." She silently followed him into the living room, and he picked up a guitar and softly played flamenco music for her. Every stroke of his fingers on the strings Clara could feel on her body. He showed her around the place, they kissed a little, and he even said, "See this room over here? This is your room." Clara was overwhelmed. She went home and was unable to see Gabriel for a month. Why? She never told him what a dreamy night she had had. She never told him how romantic it all was, how she loved the feeling of being with him, the sound of his fingers on the guitar, the incredible sensation of being played for, the deliciousness of his kiss, the sweet feeling of being in his home. Instead, she went home and started to get angry when he did not call her the next day. Furious that he didn't call the day after. So mad, actually, that when he did call, she refused to pick up the phone and refused to call him back until after she had punished him with her absence for a few more days.

Gabriel was unaware of both how much fun Clara had had with him and how angry she was with him. He knew something felt a little weird, but the night of their meeting had been so special that he persevered and asked her out again. Because he was flying to L.A. to make a presentation, he couldn't see her that week; it would have to be the following week. Clara, of course, took huge offense at this and said, all right, if you can't see me until next week, then I can't see you until the week after! Pissy, not Pussy. If Clara had once acknowledged him for their beautiful first night together, he probably would have ditched his last-minute preparations for an hour and come over right there and then to have a coffee with her. But Clara was what we call "full." She had a wonderful experience, which she did not acknowledge, so she could not receive more. This guy had swooped in and gratified a big ole desire of hers for an intensely romantic interlude, with marriage potential, and Clara was keeping all of her joy to herself.

Acknowledgment is your secret ticket into having your way in the world of men, and the world in general. Most women are wired to keep their joy to themselves, their goodies to themselves, their gratification to themselves. Women so rarely get what they want that they behave rather ungraciously when they do. Rather than an elegant "thanks," they run off with their little bag of booty and hide it under the bed, and deny it is of any value to them. This is a great disadvantage in the world of gratification. Thanks gets you more. Picture a little chipmunk at harvest time. They have these fat little chipmunk cheeks, filled with nuts. At a certain point, the cheeks are at maximum capacity. Once the nuts are swallowed, there is room in the cheeks for more. Acknowledgment is like swallowing—it makes room for more. And if you don't swallow, or acknowledge, you will throw up. Which is what Clara was doing. She had gotten such a big hunk of her dream served to her on a silver platter that night, and she never said "thanks" to Mama, to herself, to Gabriel. The purpose of acknowledgment is not to give someone else power or credit for your goodies, nor does it mean you have to share them. It is selfish. The purpose of acknowledgment is to allow *you* to have more. The more you acknowledge how sweet it is, the sweeter it gets for you.

Their affair continued, in fits and starts, as Clara began to pick up speed in her man-training experiment. Whenever she had fun with Gabriel, asked him for what she wanted, and remembered to acknowledge him, they were poetry together. One night, a few months into their relationship, they had not seen each other for a few days. Gabriel had called Clara earlier to get together, but she had a work party and so did he. He asked her, "What should I wear?' She requested his yellow sweater. That night, after her party, she had the urge to see him. She drove down his block, and there he was, walking his dog, in the yellow sweater. She pulled over. They kissed. He picked her up and carried her over the threshold. Flamenco music was blasting from the stereo. Gabriel lowered her to the floor and tangoed with her around his marble center hall, and back to the living room where he lowered her gently to the sheepskin rug in front of the fireplace. They rolled around on the floor, making out, and suddenly Clara felt overwhelmed and awful and sick to her stomach. She said she had to go, and bolted out the door. As she dashed back to her car, she remembered, "Mama says, Acknowledge. Acknowledge. Acknowledge!" Both hands pressed on the hood, she caught her breath for a moment, and then ran back to Gabriel's door and rang the buzzer. "Gabe, I just wanted to tell you that was maybe the most romantic night of my life! To run into you on the street, to have you wearing the yellow sweater like I had asked, to have you kiss me and carry me over the threshold, and dance with me, and sweep me off my feet was too amazing, too wonderful, and I will never forget it!" At this point, Clara was crying. Gabriel swept her in his arms, took her inside, and held her. They ended up talking and holding each other all night long, and Clara didn't feel overwhelmed and awful and sick to her stomach anymore. She felt like she had a friend in Gabriel because she had acknowledged him, and by so doing, made room for herself.

Creating the Right Environment for You to Flourish

We are going to cultivate your patience. Even sprouts don't sprout overnight. It takes a few days. And when a woman meets a guy, she has a bizarre tendency to abandon her world for her man. She ditches her friends, quits her normal fun activities, and becomes all about him and his world. Mama will have none of this. Keep your friends. Maintain all those cool things you did before you met him. We want you to fit him into your fabulous life, not the other way around. Sister Goddess Rae met a hot guy, Mike, who lived in Paris. She fell head over heels for him, left Chicago, left her burgeoning career as an executive in the music industry, moved to Paris, and set up housekeeping. As you can imagine, she quickly became bored and miserable. She had no friends, she didn't speak French, she had nothing to do, and when Mike would come home from his fun, rewarding day at his office, he would find her dejected, depressed, and miserable. What happened to the happy, interesting woman he fell in love with? Rae was the one who suggested that she move in with him. He only did what she asked. Of course they broke up. That's when Rae moved to New York City to do Mama Gena's School of Womanly Arts. She is returning to the beautiful, vital Rae that she was born to be.

We have read that story about the prince carrying us off to his castle so many times that we have a weird, almost primeval drive to abandon our own ship and climb aboard his, no matter what it looks like, or what direction it is going. Cut it out, darlings. You know so much more about what will make *both* of you happy than he does, even if you don't know exactly what you want to do with him. When I first met my Bruce, he was selling housewares. I went with him to a houseware convention, and as I looked around and saw all these worn-out, tacky salesmen, I thought to myself, No way. We are going to get my guy out of this field and into something fun. I don't know what exactly, but I know he will not be spending his life like *this*. And look at what a fine, beautiful adventure I cooked up for us! You really do know what's best for both of you, even if you have doubts about your desires.

Create an Island of Friendship with Your Man

Many women who have been single for a while have very close relationships with their girlfriends. They tell each other everything, discussing each date, each kiss, each touch with their current beaux. This is cool, up to a point. At a certain point, you will decide that you want to have a bit more with a particular guy. At that point, you have to train yourself to become friends with the alien. Just like you would not want your friends to go around talking behind your back, don't go around talking behind his. Don't betray the sacred secrets of your intimacy by telling your girlfriends things about him that he does not know you are sharing. Sister Goddess Gwen was dating Howard for about six months. Howard, a confirmed bachelor, had told Gwen, on the night before his thirty-fifth birthday party, that he was thinking about marrying her and having children with her. Gwen was so excited that she called her best girlfriends and her sisters to tell them what Howard had said. She neglected to tell Howard that she had done this. At his birthday party, one of her sisters went over to Howard and said, "I hear you are ready to marry my sister Gwen and have kids!" As you can imagine, Howard was incredibly hurt and upset about this, and it created a big rift in the fabric of their relationship. If you want to be his number-one friend, make him yours and treat him that way. That is going to feel the best to you anyway.

Handcuff Yourself to Your New Desires Instead of Your Old Habits

Most women expect that their guy will change, or a new guy will alter them, rather than experimenting with changing their own habits. Sister Goddess Laura had a habit of always paying for things on dates. Whoever he was, however much money he made, she was reaching into her wallet and buying movie tickets and paying dinner tabs. It never worked out with any of her guys. Why? She really didn't want to pay all the time. She just thought she had to. She thought they wouldn't want to go out with her if she didn't. Actually, the reason guys never stuck around long was that they never got a shot at making Laura happy. She would quickly do everything herself, then be mad about it. The guys would feel her resentment and disappointment with them, but alas, they were not mind readers. She did not even give them a clue as to what she wanted. It was almost like a challenge going on inside her head. If the guy couldn't figure out what it was that was going to make her happy, then fuck him, he didn't deserve her. And so on, and so on. Laura was forty-two years old and alone. When she became a Sister Goddess and realized that no man on earth could penetrate the wall she had built around herself and her desires, she wanted to see if she could experiment with creating a different outcome. On going to the movies with Bobby, her new beau, she would stuff her hands in her pockets in order to stifle her knee-jerk, grab-the-wallet-and-pay reflex. She would plan a trip to the bathroom to hyperventilate when the check came at the coffee shop. It was a big challenge for Laura to retool and allow Bobby to spoil her. "It's only an experiment!" I told her. "You can revert at any time to all your old habits. Just give this a one-month shot." At the end of the month, Laura and Bobby were still together. He even brought her flowers. This was something no man had ever done for her before. Laura was in heaven. Uncomfortable heaven, but heaven, nevertheless.

I know, I know, baby, this is a lot to absorb. So much retooling going on here. Well, as ever, Mama's got a little homework for you. Just a little reinforcement between encounters with the alien.

Exercise #1: "Biscuit Voice" and the Training Cycle

1) *The Biscuit Voice Exercise.* Do you communicate in a way that is designed to get the results you are after? My dog, Princess, used to bark her head off and take small nibbles out of guests as they entered my home. Not good. We hired a dog trainer. She told us that when we yelled at Princess for this rude behavior, we scared her further and aroused her to be even more viciously protective (she thought she was protecting us). We were taught to use "biscuit voice." We spoke to her as though we were offering her a doggy biscuit. "Good Princess, yes, you are okay, Princess, nice Princess," and so on. Most of us do not realize the level of profound anger and disapproval we normally express when we communicate. When we train ourselves to remove the doubt, hostility, and rage from our communications, we get better results and we are happier. It takes a lot out of a gal to channel all that fury. Much more fun to be adorable. Bruce and I tease each other with this biscuit-voice thing all the time. If I ever raise my voice, he will say "biscuit voice" to me, and vice versa.

2) *The Training Cycle Exercise:* There is a format of communication that will absolutely always give you the results you want from any human being, but especially your guy. It is a three-part communication cycle:

1. Approve of your guy or find something you really appreciate about him.
2. Give your man a problem, *one* problem, to solve.
3. Praise him when he accomplishes it or takes a step toward accomplishing it.

This is an example of how it could go:

1. Frank, you look so sexy in that suit.
2. Could you help me on with my coat?
3. Thanks so much.

When you practice this, it becomes second nature. It is such an improvement from the way we were taught to communicate with men: "You idiot! You never open doors for me. You never help me on with my coat! Can't you be more like Jean's husband? He does everything for her, you do nothing for me." Which style feels more pleasurable to you?

Exercise #2: Research Your Desires

Do some research. Make a list of fun experiences that a man can give you, or places that you would like to be taken, or restaurants you want to try. Here is a sample list:

1. A boat ride at sunset around the Statue of Liberty
2. A rose petal bath
3. Dinner at a Japanese restaurant

4. Tea at the Plaza
5. Tickets to *Hairspray* on Broadway
6. Lingerie shopping
7. Time spent having him shave my legs and give me a pedicure

Exercise #3: Pleasure Intensive

It is time to up the level of you pleasuring yourself. Make a little decision in your head: every time you find yourself in a situation in which you are not having fun, you will stop all action and go have some fun. For example, one of my Italian Sister Goddesses was at a party last week with her friend. Sister Goddess Greta noticed, about halfway through this party, that she was not having fun. What did she do? She went into the bathroom and self-pleasured for a few minutes. She came out a few minutes later feeling all fresh and dewy and ready to dance. She basically took over the party and flirted her ass off and caused a marvelous time for everyone. I want you to get in the habit of putting your foot down when you are not having fun, and causing fun for yourself instantly and for no reason. It takes a willingness to swing around 180 degrees at the drop of a dime.

All hell was breaking loose in my office yesterday. Rather than lose my mind, I met my sister-in-law for lunch at Barneys, and then we went to Verdura and picked out jewels for ourselves. We didn't buy any, but we had a marvelous time shopping. And it made us both feel very princessy.

Are you pleasuring yourself every day? It makes it so much more fun to train when you are hot and sassy. Here are some more ideas from Sister Goddesses:

"My sister arrived in the city today and I had a great time showing her around and taking her to one of my favorite restaurants (DB Bistro . . . mmmm). And tomorrow we're going to have lunch at Nobu, do some sightseeing, and then see a Broadway show. I'm having such fun showing off the city."

"So inspired after the O&O class that I completed the finishing touches to my bedroom and does it look great. Yeah! The trainer is still coming to the house two times a week, so I'm getting myself in better shape. I had my hair highlighted a little this afternoon, and I gave myself an almost-perfect French manicure!"

"I had orientation for school today. It was a lot of sitting and listening and not much getting to meet one another. . . . I left feeling a bit nervous and self-conscious and scared. . . . So I got back to my apartment just a little bit ago and found myself feeling disappointed that that guy I met last week hadn't called and, well, I had that overall desperation feeling. I realized I wasn't giving myself any approval, or credit for my accomplishments.

So I just stripped off my clothes and got in bed in my T-shirt and panties to stretch out and relax. I picked up Mama's book to do some reviewing and went over some of the basics, like deciding where you are right now is great and loving your flesh. . . . I spent about half an hour staring at the parts of my body that I love, like my collarbone. I have always been in love with my long fingers and wrists and I love the way the curve of my waist looks. . . . Then, feeling a whole lot better, I wrote out more on my desire list. By then I was feeling so good I even wrote myself a little love letter, confirming everything right now is perfect. It just felt so good I wanted to share with all of you!"

It is easy to pleasure yourself, as long as you have your attention on your pleasure as the primary goal. Pleasure yourselves, my loves. You are so worthy of the pleasures in life.

Exercise #4: Start with a Truth-I-Would-Never-Say Party

Get together via e-mail or in person with a group of your Sister Goddess girlfriends. The assignment is to tell each other truths that you would never, ever, ever tell a man. Have fun doing this. Maybe even share a bottle of wine to loosen your joints. Tell all. Write it down. There are two parts to this exercise, the exposure and the rereading of the list later on. Here is a sample list:

1. You don't know how I like my tea.
2. I don't like the way you kiss, or the way you make love.

3. When you pass wind in bed, it revolts me.
4. I don't like your family.
5. I am shocked by how dumb you are.
6. I am shocked by how small things set you off and make you so grumpy.
7. I don't like giving you oral sex.
8. I don't like your taste in clothes.
9. I wish you knew how I like to be pampered.
10. I want you to make more money than you do.

Leave this list in a drawer for a week, then look at it again. You would be surprised at how, once it's out and on paper, it becomes possible to say some truths you thought you could never say. And you would be surprised how sturdy men are. They can handle our truth. I once told Bruce that he was fat and that it grossed me out. The next thing I knew, he took up jogging and working out and he lost a lot of weight. My truth was motivating. He wants to make me happy, and he knows that everything I want works for him, ultimately. The truth will set you free.

Exercise #5: To Tell the Truth

Give yourself a dose of Mama's truth serum. This means that you make a little deal with yourself to tell the truth, *nicely*, and with fun, to every man you see. Just like Daphne did with the president. When you can say the truth to someone, you get to be yourself. When you get to be yourself, you end up liking the person you are with more. It's risky, but it is the only thing that will ever lead to a true partnership.

Sometimes it is a little tricky to figure out what exactly your truth is. You get so accustomed to compromising that you may be well on your way to an Italian restaurant before you realize you wanted Chinese. Or you suddenly find yourself to be a little testy and short, and then you realize it's because you didn't tell your guy that he hurt your feelings by not telling you that you look beautiful in your new dress. Be a little gentle on yourselves here, my truth tellers. Remember, this is all new, new, new. You can do a couple of things about this. First, tell your guy that your goal is to tell him the things that are on your mind, but it is new for you to include a man so intimately. Ask him, if ever he notices that you are becoming quiet, to ask you if there is anything on your mind. Tell him you might sometimes let him know after the fact, or as soon as you yourself figure it out. You can also keep a little truth journal by your bedside and write down the things that you remember you wanted to tell him, then tell him the next time you see him.

Exercise #6: The Acknowledgment

Make a list of all the guys in your life, and notice the ways that each guy has somehow served you. For example, my dad gave me life. He paid for my education. Sometimes men make a contribution to us by giving us things. Or by declining to give us things. My father refused to pay for my graduate school, and when I moved to New York after college, he and my mother expected me to support myself. That was a great gift, because I found out that I could take care of myself. Write an acknowledgment to each of the men who has made a contribution to you, and describe the contribution. If you feel like it, you can mail the acknowledgment letters. My father is eighty-five years old, and whenever I see him, I thank him for everything he did for me. It makes both of us feel good.

This exercise is great because when you notice what you have, and appreciate it, you make room to have more. And Mama wants you to have a lot more for yourself, and for your men.

Exercise #7: Video of the Week

Watch *Chasing Amy* with Joey Lauren Adams and Ben Affleck, directed by Kevin Smith. In this film, our heroine lays a whole lot of truth on her pal, and subsequent boyfriend. In fact, you might say that the *only* reason he becomes her boyfriend is that she lays a boatload of truth on him about who she is and what she wants. I am crazy for this movie, this writer, and this actress. Be inspired to tell all!

Chapter 6:

Sex and Romance

I used to be Snow White, but I drifted.
Mae West

In Mama's humble opinion, the sex part is the most important part of the relationship you're building. Why? Because if you get it right in bed, you have got a shot at the rest. Compromise in bed and you will compromise in every other area of your life. Sex becomes a metaphor for the whole relationship. If a woman is not receiving gratification in the bedroom, her role becomes one of service. Sex becomes just another expectation, another task. And y'all know how you feel about expectations and tasks—even if the pay is good, it's still no fun. A two-bit 'ho is a two-bit 'ho. This goes back to relationships built on the old male paradigm and it doesn't work. Eventually, neither the man nor the woman is happy. One of the biggest blind spots for women is female pleasure. It is not expected or pursued. It is not recognized as our birthright. If I can get you darlings to be as sassy and confident in expressing yourself in the bedroom as my five-year-old is on giving me her opinion on fashion, we have nothing to fear.

Remember me and my Guy? My ignorance and misinformation and doubt in the bedroom was ultimately what did us in. We had a marvelous sex life before we started having sex. We were like two kids, experimenting with our desire. We kissed and touched and caressed and sucked and licked and held each other. Then we decided, after a year or so of dating, that we should have "real" sex. After we began having intercourse, I changed the rules on him. I told him that what we should be doing was only having intercourse, no more of that "childish" experimental sensual exploration. Hey, I watched the same movies as you all did, and they never showed people doing hours of sensual exploration and discovery. They only showed whip-it-out-and-stick-it-in sex. So I told him that that was our new job. He was not thrilled with this. I remember once, when I was in his dorm room, I demanded some kind of performance from him, and he said, "Look, we don't have to do this *every* time we get together."

But being the film enthusiast that I was, I said, "Yes, Guy, in fact, we do." Eventually, I began to grow bored and disinterested in sex. It never even occurred to me that I could go "back" to those things that I had enjoyed doing with him, like kissing all night, or touching, holding, stroking, and so on. I was stuck in the expectations I expected of myself, and I completely ignored my desires. And then, of course, I began to doubt other things about us, about him, about me, and bye-bye Guy.

Use What You Know

And the thing is, my darlings, you know a lot more about what goes on under his hood than he knows about what goes on under yours. Most women know how to operate a penis. I said "operate," not "pleasure." We will be going into what pleasures a penis later. For now, it's important that you know that you know. In my "Mama Gena Gives It Up to Men" course, only about half of the guys can actually find the clitoris. Sometimes not half. And these men are really aware, hip, handsome, and interested in women. They are the cream of the crop that come to Mama. So I know what you are all faced with out there, and it ain't pretty. Every single one of us has ended up in bed with a guy who lacketh a clue. And the tricky part is that, much like the way men are when they are driving and lost, they do not ask for directions. They carry on as if they know where they are going and what they are doing. And we, as women, were taught to shut up and bite the bullet and pretend he knows what he's doing. So you have the perfect recipe for disaster—his ignorance and her stony silence. Grind them together and it spells no orgasm for her, and a paltry payback service-with-no-smile kind of orgasm for him. Not a slice of heaven, to be sure.

And most people's sex lives never make it to the realm of the ecstatic. Which is cuckoo, because we are wired for ecstasy. But, then, you would have to talk to each other, and say some truths to each other, and kick the legs out of the viewpoint that he should know and you should shut up. For now, understand that when he touches your vaginal opening as though he was playing a violin concerto, and you are feeling nothing and wondering when exactly he is going to get to the clitoris, know this: he thinks he is already there. There is no malice here, only ignorance. He will be grateful for eternity if you gently put his hand in the right spot and show him how to operate you. This is what one of my graduates from my men's course had to say:

> As you can imagine, I'm a changed man. Having gone through life believing I was a good lover, I'm now convinced that I sucked. Yet I'm filled with glee at prospects of life & love to come with my gigantic bag of knowledge. I actually found myself asking my mom yesterday why she never sat me down for a clitoris conversation. She said, "You never asked."
>
> A little course note: I quietly mocked how a kissing demo could possibly follow the "grand tour." I thought, Kissing, now that's something I'm great at. Wrong again, sporto. My technique has improved 500 percent to outstanding effect. And I personally found the kissing demo the most powerful turn-on of the day. Bravo, ladies. I salute you at full mast.
>
> Suffice it to say I've begun putting into practice that which I learned, from the lips on down. In a word, "magical"!
>
> Oh, and with me bopping around the office smiling like a cheshire cat, I've got a few students for you. So the question of the day is, "When's the next Mama Gena Gives It Up for the Men course?"

Along these lines, a man probably has absolutely no clue how you like to be kissed or touched. You do not have to submit to his aggressive, overly enthusiastic advances. You can gently show him how to be still and enjoy the stillness. And for the guy who is much too quiet and reticent, you can show him how to grab you and press you up against the wall sometimes.

You must not be stopped from your pleasure on account of his ignorance. And there will be ignorance. See, he is going to approach you the way his last girlfriend liked to be approached. Guys do that. They get into a groove that works, and they just want to stay there. My dad would drive an hour to a specific bread store, just for a loaf of bread, because he liked it and he was familiar with it. He did not even want to try a closer bread store—he liked what he liked. If a guy finds a restaurant he likes, he can go back there every night. It's good, so why not do it again. And again. Mama's goal is to inspire you to educate your man to become exactly the lover you want him to be. You can do this by knowing what you like and showing him exactly what makes you happy. It takes a woman who knows her way around her body, her pleasure, and her desire to teach a man to be great in bed.

You Don't Have to Be a Porn Star to Be Good in Bed

So what exactly does it take to be sassy and confident in the bedroom? Most women do not have a shot at it. Why? Most of us were taught that being good in bed means that we are supposed to deliver some kind of goods to a guy. We are supposed to give some kind of unforgettable B.J. Or fuck his brains out daily. Or have these great exploding orgasms as soon as he lays his hands on us. We expect ourselves to be like some porno film star. That our job is doing, rather than just being.

If a guy wanted a delivery, he could call UPS. If he wanted a porn star, he could rent a video. Men, as usual, want to serve. They live to serve. They want to pleasure us. They don't want a performance from you, they don't want to have to give a performance to you. Men want you to feel. They want you to enjoy every single drop of what they have to offer you. And my job is to turn you into a greedy little taker in bed. A glutton for your own self-pleasure. I want you to be downright piggy. Take everything you want to take, and then stop when you are done. Picture this: You are invited to a banquet. All this delicious food is laid out on a table, and it's all for you. What would you do? Probably you would delightedly sample everything that looked good to you. If you were feeling adventurous that day, you might even take a bite of something you had never tried before. If you didn't like it, you would discreetly remove it from your lips with a napkin and go on to the next juicy morsel, until you were full. That's how I want you to be in bed. I want you to take what you want, and leave the rest. I want you to indulge yourself as though you were at a party, just for you. Have an appetizer, an entrée, and dessert. Or, you can just pick. Remember, it's all for you, and Mama says, only clean your plate when you want to.

Regena Thomashauer

It Is Better to Receive Than to Give

How do you become an expert at receiving pleasure? Same way you become an expert at wine tasting or a gourmet with food. You experiment. You explore. You research. You taste. You see how *you* like the new flavor. You decide that you are going to become an expert in food and wine, and then you just do as much of that research as you are interested in doing. When I was in my waitressing phase, one restaurant I worked at sent me to wine school. I tasted hundreds of wines. Burgundies, Chardonnays, Cabernets, Rieslings, Champagnes. I tasted wines made of rotting grapes that tasted sweet and delicious. I tried brand-new wines that had been bottled days before, as well as truly ancient, elegant vintage wines. This part of my education has added more to my life than my years of calculus, geometry, and trigonometry. Every time I go to someone's home, I can bring a well-chosen bottle of wine. Every time I go to a restaurant, I can order a delicious glass of wine with my meal. Wine tasting is a pleasure that I was taught, and that I continue to learn about. It is a luxury that has added so much to my life.

Pleasure in any form is a luxury. We don't need caviar to live, we need food to live. But having caviar now and then can add enormous pleasure to one's life. We don't need pleasure in bed to survive as a species. Babies can be born without female orgasm. Women can live their entire lives, very successfully, without ever having one single orgasm. But pleasure in bed is a luxury that some of us simply do not want to do without. As I look back on my forty-six beautiful years, my most joyous memories are of the ecstatic moments of intimacy that I shared with a partner. I have had some gorgeous, wild, delicious, ecstatic, kick-ass gourmet sex. If there were sensual Olympics, I would get a prize. And I am prouder of that than my B.A. from Mount Holyoke. (And I am very proud of my B.A.) In bed, I have learned to take mine. I have learned to receive and give intense sensual pleasure. I know what it is like to be savored and to savor someone else. To touch and taste and experience my partner completely for my own enjoyment. To feel my divinity at the hands of another, and to feel my partner feeling his divinity through me. I have run toward my sensual fulfillment with abandon. With shamelessness. With enthusiasm. With outrageous joy.

Your Mama is a wild thing. Put her in bed with anyone, and she will get hers, and she will create unforgettable ecstasy for her partner. I want that for you, my darlings. I want to unleash your voracious appetite for sensual fulfillment. I want you to have, with your husbands and partners, what I have with Bruce, if you want. Bruce is a man who is totally committed to my pleasure. He is trained to deliver extended massive orgasm to my body. He knows how to have me come with his very first stroke. He has spent years in training for this. My pleasure has been our research project, and it has brought riches to our relationship that we could not have anticipated. It is so good with us that I keep him arm's reach away from me. Bruce and I work together and live together twenty-four hours a day, seven days a week. The only reason that this is possible, without us killing each other, is because of the pleasure we give to each other, and especially the pleasure he gives to me.

My sweet husband, Bruce, has become certified by the Drs.

Bodansky in delivering extended massive orgasm. Now that is an amazing skill for your husband to have! Imagine a guy who loves you so much that he was willing to study and become an expert in a field that is so wonderfully pertinent to you and your happiness. What that means for me is that, anytime I want, Bruce will take me to ecstatic heights of pleasure. And he loves being so accomplished. And I love the pleasure that is available to me, the pleasure that I take, and the pleasure that I give. It means that our sex life is all about friendship and fun, not about obligation or barter.

Can Any Woman Become Sexual Dynamite?

How'd you pull this off, Mama? Is it just something about you and your hot cross buns? Or do we all have the goods on irresistible? Well, we all come equally fully loaded in the department of sensuality, darlings. What it comes down to is, learn to use it or else you'll lose it. And as with any research project or new discipline, you start where you start. First and foremost, you have to be interested. Or at least, have an open mind. I wasn't particularly interested in wine tasting when I took my first course, but I am a naturally curious person, and I became more and more interested as I learned more and more things.

When I began my study of sensuality, the first thing I did was to learn about my own body. After I broke up with my Guy, I whipped through a couple of unsatisfactory affairs, then I decided to sit on the sidelines for a while. That would be a long while. Eight years. So when the pendulum swung the other way, and I started my sensual reentry, I leapt with great abandon. I moved into a sex commune. I began to self-pleasure, a practice I had not really explored much in my life. From the mountains to the prairies to the oceans white with foam, I gave in to whatever whim I had and whatever dalliance I desired. And the keys to the queendom were the sensual exercises and self-exploration that I am going to give you for homework at the end of this chapter. I want you to become experts at yourselves. I want you to know your every nook and cranny, and how to drive your nooks and crannies to a high state of frenzied pleasure.

Don't Put an Egg Timer on Your Orgasm

Just as we had to shake ourselves loose from the myth of the prince coming to sweep us off our feet, we have to shake ourselves loose from the myth of what an orgasm is. I find that many women who come to Mama have this idea that their pussies are wrong and their orgasms are wrong. Women feel that if they don't have an orgasm in two minutes, they are too slow. If they are not spraying ejaculate all over the room, they are dried out. If they can't find their G-spot, they are undersexed. And if they don't have orgasms during intercourse, they are frigid. Yikes, gals! How we gonna party from there? A few deep, cleansing breaths, please. . . . If you have a pussy, you have all the equipment you need to keep yourself abundantly happy and a world of men ecstatic for centuries. We have to begin to provide our pussies with the environments for growth that pussies respond to. If you wanted to grow a tomato plant, you wouldn't put it in the closet, right? You can't bake a pie in the refrigerator, true? And a pussy cannot flourish, unfold, engorge, lubricate, and feel with abandon when she is being disapproved of, judged, or criticized. Mama wants to give you some alternatives to self-criticism.

When I first began to take control of my sensual life, I began with a hand mirror. I noticed that, for most of my life, I had never paid much attention to myself physically, except, of course, to approve or disapprove of my weight or my appearance. The pleasure between myself and myself was new to me. I was quite surprised when I could receive pleasure from the curves of my back, the shape of my neck, the folds and colors of my vulva. And of course, it makes sense. You can't teach someone to appreciate a good wine unless you yourself appreciate it. We expect these guys to magically ignite us into sexual athletes when we have spent our lives as couch potatoes. Approval of yourself is free. Just like disapproval. But you have to haul your potatolike self off the couch and make the decision to approve. It requires more effort than disapproval. But then, you have to ask yourself, why give free rent in your head to a thought that takes so much away from your ability to enjoy yourself and your partner? In her wonderful book *Woman* Natalie Angier says that "sex researchers have found that women who are easily and multiply orgasmic have one trait in common: they take responsibility for their pleasure. They don't depend on the skillfulness or mind-reading abilities of their lovers to get what they want." Why not become one of those women who has her way in bed? Especially since it's up to you, not the guy, anyway. Adopt your stray pussy. Give it a good home. Nurture it. Educate it. You will give yourself a friend for life.

Care and Feeding

Congratulations. The adoption papers are complete. Your new arrival is here. What do you do first? Same as a baby. Just look at her and coo with appreciation and delight. She loves that. You can do that for a really long time, she won't mind. You may even notice she responds to your cooing by getting more engorged or lubricating or flushing with more color. This is all good. I don't know about you, but if I have a guy gazing at my pussy, cooing with joy over my beauty, I am deliriously happy. I am in no rush to have him move on to greener pastures. For me, this is better than dinner and a movie. Keep this move in your repertoire, if you like. Then we can move on to touching. Check out your fabulous goods. Keep cooing, just the same as we do when we see the miraculously small ten fingers and ten toes of a newborn. We don't demand that the kid does any heavy lifting to prove her effectiveness; we just enjoy the miracle of it all. As you check out your beautiful, miraculous self, you are not permitted to do anything but appreciate your own beauty and notice what your pussy is feeling. You are not allowed to judge. You are not allowed to press. You are not allowed to demand. You are not allowed to rush. You have to move at the speed of pussy. Look at her. Watch her. Begin to feel what she is feeling.

Set Her Free or You Will Never Be Free

This is my only ultimatum, I promise. If you do not fall head over heels in love with your pussy, exactly as she is, appreciating her exactly as she is, you will never be free to love another. Your pussy is your gal guide to being a woman. To be happy, you are going to have to live by her rules. The world of the feminine is who you are, and most women are in such heavy judgment of themselves and disapproval of themselves because they are trying to live by the male standard, and they never measure up. Pussy can set you free to appreciate, to enjoy, to feel, to experience pleasure, to trust your instincts, to say yes at the right moment and no at the right moment. She is your higher power. If you surrender to her, she will lead you to the sex life you always wanted, the intimacy you crave, the adventure of a lifetime. If you keep thinking that someone else is going to lead you to your dreams or that some man is going to take you where you want to go, you will stay forever in the purgatory of doubt, disapproval, and anger. Pussy will set you free. First you have to set her free.

Free Touching

Most people learn to touch as a way of creating a result. Know what I mean? You touch your partner to make his body feel good, right? That's one style. I call that "results touching." You are touching to produce a result in someone. That's one way to do it, but it is not the most pleasurable way. In fact, it's kind of a drag because it means there is judgment in the act itself. You touch, but you are looking for some kind of result or outcome to make sure that you were effective. In fact, your enjoyment is based on the other person's response.

You may even be touching to get that person to touch you back. That would be reciprocal touching. It means that as you touch a guy, you are working up a reciprocal bill that he owes you at the end of the experience, and he probably doesn't even know it. Too complex, too many strings attached. Even when you touch your own self that way, you are judging. You touch and you think, Hmm, that didn't feel as good as it felt last time. Or, hmm, that didn't feel as good as I expected it to feel. Not good enough for pussy. I want you to try a more selfish style of touching—free touching. Like the way you would touch a little kitten. You absent-mindedly stroke the fur. Why? It feels good to your fingers. Or when you are lying on a sheepskin rug or wearing your fur coat, you absentmindedly run your fingers through the fur. Why? It feels nice on your hand. I want you to practice free touching. Touch your hand, your hair, your skin, just for the pleasure you can give your own self. I remember the first time I ever did this, I sat it my cute little *That Girl* apartment by candlelight, in front of my mirror, and I thought, "Shit—I am beautiful! And I feel so good!" I was head over heels for myself. I touched myself from my hair, ears, eyes, neck, to my tiny little toes. And everywhere in between. I felt a little silly over how ecstatic I could make myself feel, but I mostly felt thrilled with my sensations, and decidedly and delightedly free. I was in control of my ecstasy for the very first time in my life. My ability to have joyous pleasure did not depend on a guy, it depended on me getting up off my own ass and giving it to myself. I was free. The next week, I met my wonderful husband, Bruce. I know that was made possible by my discovery of myself.

When you think you need a man to make you happy or give you pleasure or turn you on or provide orgasms, it is repulsive to a man. You are behaving as if you are a slave and an addict. And you are neither. You are a Goddess. Need implies lack or insufficiency. Relationships based on need never make it, because it is a lie. We don't "need" anything. Life is a gift, relationships are a gift, hey, even breathing is a gift. If you behave as though you are in desperate need of a man to live, you are heading for doom, repulsion, and disaster. It's gross when someone says they need you. It's attractive when they say they want you or desire you. If you find yourself attractive, you will attract any man you wish. If you find yourself desirable, every man will desire you. A woman, in the revolutionary act of loving herself, is a completely irresistible thing. Set those pussies free, gals. You are the only ones who can.

Free Sex

The consequences of freedom are so much fun. When you no longer need a man, you have the exquisite experience of your own desire. You can actually be pleasured by one. Pleasure at your fingertips—it is always there for you. Yesterday I had a free hour, 11 to 12 in the morning. I invited my husband to meet me in the bedroom. He lit some candles, put on some music, and we had a delicious, fabulous roll in the hay. It was free, friendly sex. We did everything we wanted to do with great relish. It cost nothing. It was legal. And we ended up having a marvelous day together, flirting and feeling fine. I want that for you. To have the same freedom with your sensuality as my five-year-old has at a restaurant. She orders only french fries with the same abandon as she orders a lobster. It is purely based on her desires. She does not worry about the price, she does not worry about all the food groups, she just goes for what she wants with relish. I want you to be that way in bed, and that way with your men. I want you to touch him like you are learning to touch yourself, purely for your pleasure. Don't give pleasure to him unless it's absolutely necessary for your pleasure to do so. It's a bit of rewiring I am asking for here, I know. I deal with countless women who spent their teens, twenties, thirties, and so on, giving payback blow jobs in the backseats of taxis or payback fucks in return for dinner, a date, or to simply get that asshole off their back. These gals never get to experience pleasure, because all their sex is about reciprocity or manipulation. I want you, my darlings, to have the experience of free sex. Free touching. Free sensuality. Free sex. I want you to make all your sensual decisions from your desires, not your obligations. I don't care if that means that all you do for the next ten years is lie down, spread your legs, and have your guys give you orgasms and you never touch them. You deserve it. You and your sisters have spent thousands of years in the service business. You have quite a lot of coming to do to catch up with the guys or, more specifically, to fill yourselves up from your pleasure deficit. Believe me, there will be a day, if you are a true student of your pleasure, that you will be filled up. You will be overflowing with sensual goodness and gratitude if you allow your desires to be your guide. Don't do anything you don't want to do. Only do the things you want to do. If you are vigilant about going only for your pleasure, you will reconstruct yourself into a Goddess in the bedroom. You will set your sensuality free. And you will lay a life-changing piece of ass on the guy next to you, especially if that guy has been attentive to you and in service of your pleasure.

Most people have never experienced sex from that perspective. They think that payback sex, reciprocal sex, obligatory sex, mercy sex is as good as it gets. When all you've had is Kmart sex, you think it is the only way to go. I want you, my darlings, to have Harry Winston sex, Manolo Blahnik sex, Mount St. Helens sex, thunder and lightning sex, interplanetary sex, 40,000-leagues-under-the-sea sex. And any other kind of sensual ecstasy that your heart and pussy desire. And free pussies are the only launching pad for a lifetime of sensual pleasure. Give her her day in the sun. You won't be sorry. I get phone calls and e-mails constantly from all my Free Pussy Sister Goddesses, saying, "Thank you, Mama! I never knew how sweet it could be." I want to hear that from you. For you. Let me know how sweet it is.

Letters from the Front, or, Training Him

How do you become expert in receiving pleasure? Is it interesting for a man to spend a lot of time giving pleasure to a woman? And how do you become equally skilled at giving pleasure? Is there some kind of special stroke or special sex act that men find just irresistible? What does it take to become intoxicating in bed? Is it the meat? Is it the motion? Do only some gals got it? Can a guy spot it from across a crowded room? And can a Sister Goddess find happiness with a man who can't even kiss well? What if he doesn't seem to know about the clitoris? Is there hope? Oh, my darlings, Mama has much to say about your sex life, She wants a lot for you in this department and won't rest until you get it exactly your way. The bottom line is, if a woman is going to compromise about the way a man kisses her or touches her, she will end up divorcing him. If you can get the sex thing right—really, really, really right—then you have the potential to take your man and turn him into a hero. Here are some letters from fellow Sister Goddesses, in the trenches of training.

Dear Mama,

After a lifetime of being a couch potato, I'm starting to pleasure myself. I'm finding myself adorable, and I'm loving myself. Now I have a really cute but clue-less man in my life. He doesn't even know how to kiss. He kisses like a starved Great Dane and I'm the first meal he's had in weeks. What do I do? Flush him and find another? We really have fun together when we are not in bed.

Love,
Hot, throbbing, and dripping

Dear Hot,

Good show, babe. Mama is proud. You can see the prince inside a frog! You have to remember that you are not the only one who has been a lifetime couch potato. This perfectly nice guy you have found was never taught anything worth knowing about how to pleasure a woman. He has had the same insufficient training as you. Cut him some slack and put him in your pleasure boot camp. You may feel you don't know much, but it's a helluva lot more than he knows. When I first met Bruce, I had to teach him how to kiss. He has never forgotten, and he gets better and better every day.

Your ever lovin',
Mama

Dear Mama,

How?

Love,
Hot

Dear Hot,

Good question. When you feel turned on and full of fun, tell him you really want to kiss him. Explain to him that you have this really fun way that you like to kiss and you wondered if he would let you show him. He will say yes. Tell him not to move a muscle, you will do everything. Then you can sit on his lap, or next to him, and very gently kiss his cheeks, his ears, his neck. Enjoy the smell of him, the taste of him, and tell him so as you are kissing him. Then, slowly and gently, kiss his lips. Tell him not to move. As you get more and more turned on, you can open your lips a little and gently use your tongue in an exploratory way. You can eventually penetrate his mouth with your tongue. He continues to remain still, tongue inside his mouth. The goal here is for you to move slowly and to relish every drop of this, not just to plunge your tongue down his throat so you can prove how wild and sexy you are. If you want him to feel you and pay attention to you, you are going to have to teach him to do that by feeling him and enjoying every drop of him. Less is more in kissing. As you get more and more turned on, use more tongue and penetrate his mouth more. You lead, he follows. When I teach men to kiss in my "Mama Gena Gives It Up to Men" class, I have two Sister Goddesses sit up in front of the room, on the stage, and kiss each other. The Sister Goddesses love to impart wisdom in this fashion, and the men are in awe. Most guys have no idea how to really feel and savor every drop of the sensation. Women know. And it is a great pleasure for us to lead them into the world of more and more feeling.

Love,
Your Man-Training Mama

P.S. Rome, as they say, was not built in a day. Be prepared for it to take you a few weeks to complete your Kissing Recovery Program. Enjoy the incremental progress he makes. You will get him to the promised land, step by step. Praise him for every tiny drop of progress he makes.

Dear Mama,

I met this guy who is absolutely crazy about me. Last night he said that all he wanted to do was give me pleasure. He spent hours stroking me and kissing me all over. It made me nervous because I am not used to so much attention, and I don't want him to get bored. When I would try to do something to him while he was touching me, he wouldn't let me. He said he just wanted to enjoy me. Is it really pleasurable for a man to give a woman pleasure all night long? I could hardly enjoy myself because I was so afraid I was boring him.

Nervously yours,
Worried in Utah

Dear Worried,

Panic ye not! There is no object more worthy of worship than the body of a woman! Painters have spent their lives painting us, sculptors sculpting us, poets writing verse for us, "Shall I compare thee to a summer's day?" asked Shakespeare. The Goddess, which is you, invites worship. By permitting a man to worship at your shrine, you give him the gift of a lifetime, and a most memorable night. Keep doing your pleasure exercises. The more you worship at your own shrine, the more you will understand the gift of rapture that you are. And the more you understand the gift that you are, the more you will understand the great honor you bestow upon a man whom you permit to pleasure you. It takes a while to elevate yourself in your own eyes. You are building up your pleasure muscle here. Tell him that you are nervous and that while you love his attention, this is all new for you. Don't be afraid to tell him when you have had enough. When you find you are no longer feeling anymore, just worrying, don't yell, "Stop!" Instead, see if you can muster a friendlier "Wow, that was so amazing, and I am so full with pleasure! Let's take a break for a little while." He will be happy that he did his job well. Men like to know they have accomplished their goal: pleasuring us. Lying back and receiving pleasure is new for many women. Most of us were trained to serve. Take it slow. But I will tell you this, men run after women who permit men to pleasure them, and men run away from women who spend their time trying to pleasure men.

With an oooh *and an* aaaaah *and a sis boom baaah,*
Mama

Dear Mama,

I have been married for five years, and to tell you the truth, I get bored and tired about halfway through intercourse sometimes. I just want him to be done, and then I start to get irritated. Can't they come faster?

Signed,
Too pooped to party

Dear Pooped,

Let me ask you a question. If you and I went out to eat together, and we ordered appetizers and then entrées, and then I got full halfway through my entrée, would you insist that I eat every scrap of food on my plate? I don't think so. You would probably permit me to stop when I was full and take home a doggie bag if I wanted. It's the same thing with sex. You are the one who made up the rule that once he starts, he has to finish the job. It's not really true. A man has had a really good day if he gets his cock hard that day. He doesn't need to have an orgasm every time his cock gets hard, and he doesn't have to come every time he has intercourse. If all you want is one delicious stroke of him inside you, have it and then stop. You can do other fun things. You can watch him do himself. You can touch him with your hand or mouth. Or you can enjoy that one exquisite stroke of him inside you, and you can roll over and go to sleep. The important thing is, don't do anything you don't want to do—otherwise, you will be angry at him and less inclined to be enthusiastic about more sensual encounters with him. And you know what, Pooped? Sometimes Mama gets so hungry that she orders two entrées and eats every single bite and licks the plate clean. Know what I mean? So, hold the pickles, hold the lettuce, special orders don't upset us. Have it your way. It's the absolute only way to unleash your full-throttle enthusiasm, which is what we all want unleashed.

Bon Appétit,
Mama

Dear Mama,

Any tips for a great B.J.?

Love,
Hot Lips

Dear Lips,

Let's take a precautionary moment. If you are single and shopping, I want to introduce you to a Sister Goddess's best friend: latex protection. All of my Sister Goddesses have a creed: our orgasm comes first, before his, and we always, always use protection. When Mama made her great reentry to the world of dating, she had a big advantage: She knew she had no communicable diseases. Wanting to remain as pure as the driven snow, Mama packed her latex gloves, Saran Wrap, and condoms in her purse as she went about the business of exploring her sensuality. She used a latex or plastic barrier whenever she was encountering semen or saliva. You would be surprised how free a gal can feel to unleash her lust when she knows she is not risking a shred of her physical well-being. If a guy did not wish to cooperate, then he did not have the privilege of being with Mama. But you know what? I never had a guy turn me down. Resist, maybe, but never refuse. And you can feel everything through a thin layer of latex. In fact, you can sometimes feel even more because you are paying such close attention. Worry diminishes pleasure far more than a thin latex barrier. It feels so much sexier when you know the guy is looking out for his health, and yours. So that is Step One of a good B.J. Protection. Step Two: if you want to be really good at this, you have to do it for only one reason—your pleasure. It only feels good if you lick and suck for your fun and fulfillment. If you try to perform or act sexy or be like a porn star, it feels mechanical. You don't eat ice cream to serve the cone. You don't lick a lolly to make the pop happy. You do it all for you. Using his cock to pleasure your mouth and tongue is the best way to drive him to ecstasy. The best way to give pleasure is to take pleasure. What a good deal.

With love and latex,
Mama

Dear Mama,

This may be a first for you. I have been married for twenty-three years and have three beautiful children and a great husband. It wasn't until I read your book last year that I ever looked at my pussy. I come from a culture where we do not discuss these matters. It wasn't until I read that chapter that I ever knew I had a clitoris. So I am thinking that not only do I want to enjoy my discovery, but I want my husband to enjoy it, too. Can you teach an old dog new tricks? I am thinking I am the old dog.

Signed,
Unleashed and Awaiting Further Instructions

Dear Unleashed,

Congratulations on your brave discovery. Many women go whole lifetimes without ever finding the controls to their pleasure dial. I have had women in my classes who have been married forty years and never knew they had a clitoris. I have had young women in their twenties with the same complaint. Clitorises are so ridiculously responsive and loaded with nerve endings that they never atrophy. With a little encouragement, they come to full raging life. Your job is to share your beautiful discovery with your husband. You can tell him what you have just learned and ask him if he wants to see it. If he says yes, you can sit up on the arm of the couch while he lies on it, and spread your legs and show him. You can also demonstrate for him what you have learned about how it likes to be touched. Have you heard of music-appreciation classes and art-appreciation classes? You can give him, and yourself, a clitoris-appreciation class. Go slowly. If you want some assistance on your journey, both of you can read *Extended Massive Orgasm* and *The Illustrated Guide to Extended Massive Orgasm,* both by Drs. Vera and Steve Bodansky. You can also come to New York and take their workshop. They taught me and my husband everything we know about pleasure, and we have a gorgeous sex life and an absolutely wonderful marriage. All because we learned how to pleasure our clitoris. It's never too late.

> *More to come,*
> *Love,*
> *Mama*

Exercise #1: To Thine Own Self Be True

Most women expect their man to be a sexual Olympian on the first date. Any man can become a sexual Olympian, but it requires practice, practice, practice. Step One of practice has nothing to do with the guy. Mama is a firm believer that Sleeping Beauty must awaken herself. Just like on the dance floor—he has a better shot at making you look like Ginger Rogers if you have done a bit of shaking your booty before he got there. Step One: get your fine self some privacy, get your clothes off, and let's begin, one limb at a time, to see exactly what kind of pleasure we can extract from you. You may want to set the stage a bit by lighting some candles and putting on some music. It's always good to seduce yourself. Then get yourself up on your bed and start by very lightly touching the palm of your hand. Do little circles in your palm with the other hand. Feels good, no? Try other strokes—tapping, pressing, fingernail traces. The goal is to awaken as much pleasurable sensation in your palm as in the whole wonderful rest of your body. We are going to do this lovely exercise for twenty minutes a day until you know what kind of stroke you like on your inner thigh versus your outer thigh, how you like your hair stroked, your wrists caressed, and so on. It's a gorgeous, sensual body, and your knowledge of what pleasures it is the key to having a rich, luxurious sensual life.

Exercise #2: In Honor of Sister Goddess Doctor Jocelyn Elders

Mama wants you to apply that same little look and touch from Exercise #1 to your pussies. Put on your little research caps, my Girl Scouts, and let's head into the bush.

Exercise #3: Reading Assignments

Read *The Illustrated Guide to Extended Massive Orgasm* by Drs. Vera and Steve Bodansky, the leading experts in the emerging field of female orgasm. If you can follow a recipe on a box of cake mix, you can teach yourself and your partner to have extended massive orgasms. It's not the meat, it's the motion.

Mama's thought is, darlings, if you get the sex bit right, you can get the whole man-training bit right. Why? Sex is a subtopic of communication. And if you can communicate in bed, you can communicate anywhere. As usual, serving Queen Pussiah will lead you to every one of your dreams. You gotta serve her, and then so will he. There is only one thing that can spoil your journey . . . doubt.

Chapter 7

Mechanical Failures, His and Hers

It requires infinitely greater genius to make love, than to make war.

Ninonde Lenclos,
seventeenth-century courtesan

In spite of your best intentions, in spite of having read this book cover to cover, in spite of pleasuring yourself seventeen times a day and buying yourself flowers and acknowledging your panties off, and doing forty-nine daily sessions of spring cleaning on men, every once in a while, your self-training is going to fly out the window. All of your relationships will suffer. The Anger Fairy is gonna bite you on the butt and you are going to chew the head off any man, woman, or child in your vicinity. You will feel possessed. Like an attack dog. An impromptu audition for the Wicked Witch of the West, or Medea, the Sequel.

Men are the logical target for all this inequity. Anger is the largest issue between men and women in our world today. And I am gonna ask something rather extreme of you, given the current prevailing circumstances. Don't go there.

I find that most women I meet are just flat-out annoyed with guys. Their state of annoyance is second nature to them, so they don't see it is as an issue. These women may not even register their anger as anger. They behave as if they are unfortunate victims. Other women are having fun in relationships and getting their goals, but poor me, I can't attract a guy, I can't meet a guy, I can't keep a guy. Anyone who feels lacking in some way, anyone who feels that other women have more advantages, anyone who says "poor me" is actually a dangerously angry woman. Dangerous to herself and to others. Dangerous to herself because she won't take the responsibility to go after her goals and love her life. Dangerous to others because she will always blame other people for her insufficiency. You gotta seriously watch out for this kind of gal. And she is everywhere. You can't walk down the street without bumping into thousands of her. It's kind of like the way cigarette smoking was in the 1950s and '60s. Everyone was doing it, so we couldn't believe it was killing us. Anger is the smoking of the twenty-first century. Most people believe they have a right to be angry about whatever it is they are angry about. But anger just gives you wrinkles. And it won't deliver a great sex life or love life or fun in any form. So I am encouraging you to look at your options.

When you were six months old, you giggled every time anyone tickled you or made eye contact with you. You were easy in those days. You gave it up for anyone. Give it up for yourself, now. The only reason why you won't is because you are angry. You are angry because some women seem to be cuter than you or some women seem to have better breaks than you or some women are younger or thinner or have more money than you. You are angry because you have too many mouths to feed and you don't make a lot of money. You are angry because you work too hard and get so little in return. Men have beaten you and cheated on you and left you. Men you have wanted haven't wanted you. You are angry because life has not turned out like that fairy tale they promised you. And you know what, darlings, your anger is justified. You have been sold a bill of goods that has no bearing on reality, and you have no shot at never-ending happiness. If we were at the pearly gates and all the archangels were presiding over your trial, they would all agree that you had been swindled. You got a bum deal. A lemon. You have every right to be pissed off. And you know what Mama says? Tough titties, girlfriends.

All the justifiable anger in the world is not going to get you a drop of happiness. It is not gonna get you that piece of ass you want or that man you want or that baby you are interested in having. All your anger is gonna get you is more anger. And what's worse, you are so accustomed to being angry that you don't even know you are angry. You haven't breathed an unangry breath for years.

Anger is not forever. It is simply a decision that you make that has consequences, just like pleasure is a decision that you make that has consequences. If you feel angry about something, quit gardening. You don't want to accidentally hack away a rosebush just because you are having a hissy fit. Nothing good will ever come from any actions taken in anger. Anger screws up communication. You are the biggest victim when you are angry, and you are also at your weakest. I keep bringing this up because it is my Achilles' heel. I feel so self-righteous when I get mad at Bruce that I am like the Queen of Hearts, screaming, "Off with his head!" You can imagine how adorable I am at a moment like that. Anger is a cheap thrill. Anger destroys. Remember my friend Chef? Chef was such an angry guy that he gave himself a heart attack and died at the age of thirty-six. I miss that man in so many ways. The seductive part is, you feel so divinely self-righteous as you scream and rage. The problem is, once your outburst is over, you feel like shit. And you have a huge bill to pay in order to ingratiate yourself with the person you just blasted. Because of my wild temper, I am familiar with all forms of groveling. I have apologized on my knees to Bruce, to my friends, with Academy Award tears, flowers, and poetry. Ultimately, there is no form of apology that is more effective than holding my fiery tongue and finding a way to communicate what I want nicely. And that is the price, the price of entry into the world of relationships. It feels as if it costs you everything; every drop of ego must be surrendered at the gates. But you know what? You always have more ego. And what you get in return is a shot at partnership, and the privilege of loving and being loved. And just like gardening, you have to tend yourself and your seedlings each and every day. Or else they don't grow.

First, let's find out how high you read on the anger meter.

The How-to-Tell-If-You-Are-Pissed Quiz

Please answer true or false to the following questions:

1. You find yourself to be short-tempered or impatient with people who commit small infractions.
2. When you see a man smile at you or catch your eye, you feel disgusted or annoyed.
3. When someone says, "Smile, it's a beautiful day!" you want to kick them.
4. You feel overburdened, overworked, rushed. If someone were to ask you for one more thing, you would scream.
5. You are revolted by a guy who wears a toupee or otherwise tries to conceal a bald spot, who dresses "snazzy," who wears cowboy boots, or who has large jewelry.
6. You have a long list of qualifications for a man, and no guy seems to measure up.
7. Many of your girlfriends are prettier, more attractive to men, and have better men than you.

If you had a high score on the anger quiz, I want to encourage you to go back to Mama 101 and read *Mama Gena's School of Womanly Arts* again, and this time, do *all* the pleasure exercises with enthusiasm. If we don't get you aggressive about your fun to the same degree that you are aggressive about men, we won't be able to get you to give it up. I promise you will not *want* to do this. Do it anyway. I want the guys to have a shot at making you happy.

You and I are going to have our little showdown right here, right now, in this chapter. You are not going to like how much depends on your ability to be adorable. You are just not used to being adorable all that much of the time. You are exquisite at it, in spurts. Put on a new dress, some fresh lipstick, and you are as cute as a button and sweet as pie. If I zoomed in on you some fine morning when you were feeling cranky and bloated and angry at your boss and tired of your routine, annoyed with the dog, sick unto death of your commute, pissed at your mother, broke, and feeling sorry for yourself, and I interviewed you on your opinion about men, we would have to burn the tape with your response. Destroy the evidence. Run for the hills. And most of us don't realize how we run our engines on this low-level cranky speed most of the time. Those of you who are reading these words and saying, "Oh, that doesn't apply to me" are the worst offenders. "Offenders" is too strong a word. The "unadorables" is a better choice. The "unadorables" are a pretty distinct group. They encompass the majority of women all over the world. If you do not teach a woman to adore herself from the top of her head to the tips of her toes, she won't. And since she knows, somewhere deep inside, that being adored is an essential activity, she will spend the rest of her life from low-grade annoyed to high-grade angry that she is not adored. This woman will be right, and she will be alone. She may have friends who watch her tumble through life, but she won't have a main man squeeze. She will have buddies who all have similar complaints, a few pals who want to rescue her but, essentially, she won't get off her crankiness long enough to have a love affair that can lead anywhere fabulous. She will have kind of disappointing, tortured love affairs, in which the guys don't come all the way through—they always disappoint.

Sometimes women join the ranks of the temporarily unadorable. From Princeton, New Jersey, Sister Goddess Irene was fifty-something and married for just five years, to her second husband. After her divorce a few years back, she really got her life together. She had a job that she loved and that challenged her, as well as a lively group of friends. She took great care of herself and her two teenage daughters, and she really appreciated every single day and the opportunity to be herself and start her life over again. Optimum man-meeting time. You start to love yourself, adore yourself, enjoy yourself, and you will have men trailing after you wherever you go. There is no aphrodisiac sweeter than a woman who finds herself to be irresistible. Well, Sister Goddess Irene found a guy. This man was great. They had fun and had so much in common. The only problem—he was in the middle of a divorce. And when his wife found out he was dating, she made things very hard for him. For the next two years, he went to court over custody issues, money, property, and so on. Irene was by his side for every battle, slowly wearing herself out. His angst was her angst. Plus her angst was her angst. She stopped doing things with her friends, stopped treating herself well, stopped enjoying her work. She was overtaken by the trials of the trials. That's when she came to Mama. Fortunately, she knew that her wells were dry and she needed to do a little something to get herself up, running, and frothy again, so she put herself in pleasure boot camp. Thing is, you can't ever leave pleasure boot camp. You have to live there if you want to be adorable. Which, of course, you all do.

There are some of you who just run a perpetual low-grade crankiness, like Epstein-Barr syndrome. Your overall malaise is hard to pin down, hard to quantify, hard to predict. Some days you feel okay, some days not, but it seems like you feel like yourself, just cranky. You are so accustomed to this feeling that you don't even notice its absence, or its presence. Crankiness is your way of life. It's so many people's way of life that it is difficult to identify. This was my lifestyle, cranky-assed bitch. I was the lead singer in the Unadorables. It was a way of life. I remember when I first started to date my husband, I wouldn't ask him for things, I would whine. A simple "Can we get together this weekend?" would ring with high notes of complaint. How could a guy succeed with me if he was already disappointing me before we even started? Fortunately, I was stopped in my tracks by J.B. and Laura. They heard my complaints about Bruce not doing this, not doing that, not being this, not being that, and they cautioned me to improve my tone or lose my man. Which hit me like a ton of bricks because I never knew I was coming across like a shrew. I thought I was being as precious as a slice of lemon meringue pie. Other people were cranky, I was a little sweetheart, in my own mind. Other people, especially Bruce, just weren't coming up to my modest standards. I wasn't being overbearing! I wasn't being demanding! Tee-hee. I had five thousand years of whining women, training me to join their ranks. And so many kinds of whining to choose from! Quiet, withholding whines. Loud, vulgar ones. Abusive four-letter whines. Subversive "it's *fine,* really" whines. "Why does she have it and I don't" whines. Oh, I guess you could call me a whine connoisseur. I whined when he was late, whined when he was early. I whined because even if he did what I wanted, it wasn't exactly the way I would have done it. And of course, I was the leading authority in all matters pertaining to all things. Bruce really liked me, and he was doing his best to make me happy, but I was a real pain in the ass. And I am proud of what a big pain I was, and am. Because if a pain-in-the-ass, opinionated whine connoisseur such as myself could get herself a partner in life and develop a love affair like I have, there is hope for every woman who is interested. And the cool part is, you will have much more fun playing this game than you are currently having. It will cost you more because as I see it, the man/woman game is the costliest game in town. Not because it's expensive with dollars and cents, but because it costs you ego. You know ego—it's that opinion of yourself that you spent years forming. Hey, I was thirty-three years old when I met Bruce, and I spent thirty-three years cultivating the exact level of crankiness that I lived by. Crankiness was my creed. It was my M.O. I was known for it. And I had to give that up to have fun with a man. It seemed a big sacrifice at the time, and it still does.

Most women have been trained to experience their doubt more strongly than their desire or vision. That's what makes us so cranky all the time. And there is an antidote to doubt. It's like this, to be perfectly blunt: trust your pussy or trust your doubt. Most women I meet have complete and total faith in their doubt. It is unshakable. That's why their lights are off and they have no glow. They doubt that they are gorgeous, fabulous, incandescent, inspired, and basically pussalicious. They believe they are wrong in some major, irrefutable way. When a Sister Goddess chooses to doubt herself, it has remarkably destructive consequences in her own life and in the lives of everyone around her. When a Sister Goddess makes the decision to go for fun, it has remarkably magical consequences in her life and in the lives of everyone around her.

We will examine the consequences to a Sister Goddess, and her men, when she chooses to doubt herself rather than celebrate herself. And, my darlings, there is not a Sister Goddess among us, your Mama included, who won't circle the drain of doubt at least a dozen times a day. You can't stop it from appearing in your head—it's what you do about it that is relevant. You are not wrong for doubting. You are not wrong for succumbing to your doubts. What I want to do is simply give you some more pleasurable alternatives.

Some women hear the voice of doubt, and they allow it to kill their desires. Some women hear the voice of doubt and they hold even tighter to their dreams. I had an amazing illustration of that fact yesterday. One of my clients, Sister Goddess Patty, a forty-four-year-old physician, came to me in a veil of tears. She had been dating a guy for two years, never wanting to really commit to him, never really sure he was the One. She was unwilling to break up with him or to tell him of her true desire to have a baby. All she did was doubt and fret. She hadn't heard from him in a month. He just sort of went away, retreating into work, unwilling to see her. She felt he was perhaps her last chance at happiness, but she had neither gone for it, nor let him go. She was, once again, alone with her doubt. Sometimes we have to learn each of our life lessons the hard way. Later that morning, I went shopping and ran into another client, Sister Goddess Sarah. She was pushing a baby stroller with her beautiful one-month-old daughter in it. She was forty-four years old and had decided to just fucking go for it with this crusty but wonderful man, Ken. She had spent her life in the land of doubt and decided to simply experiment with the land of going for fun and unleashing her desires with a man. She figured it was last call, so she might as well order a cocktail. Can you see how doubt can squeeze the life out of a desire? And how desire has a life of its own? Would Cleopatra have become a legend if she had doubted her beauty and power? Would FDR have had three terms (elected four times!) if he had not had Eleanor by his side? Could Helen of Troy have turned the heads of an entire army if she had believed there was such a thing as a bad hair day? Could Clinton have managed his last year in office without Hillary holding firmly to the reins? It is such a magnificent sight to see a woman in her flat-out glory, and such a sad sight to see a woman in bondage to her doubt of her flat-out glory. The more powerful we become, the more powerful everyone who has the privilege of being in our vicinity becomes.

Sister Goddess Lucy is a very successful singer/songwriter of rising fame. She is wildly successful in every department of her life except men. She has a house in Martha's Vineyard, a loft in SoHo, cars, clothes, shoes, and so on. She says she wants a guy now. She actually has a man, Teddy, that she is very interested in. He is a musician, as she is. He calls her whenever he gets a chance, but he is a busy man with his own flourishing career. He recently came back from a tour in Europe. She knew he was back in town but refused to call him, and he didn't call her. One day, her single friend Annie called her, and said, "Hey Lucy, have you heard from Teddy? You know he's been back in town for two weeks. You might as well face it, he's not interested in you." Well, that was all Lucy needed. She called Teddy's answering machine about a hundred times, leaving him desperate messages, crying as she drank a bottle of wine, alone. She called her ex-boyfriend, Mark, and sobbed, asking him, "Why did you leave me?" She basically accepted Annie's invitation and took a fabulous swan dive into the murky waters of doubt.

The next day, Lucy called Mama. We had a good laugh at her dramatic nature, and agreed that she had definitely chosen the right career for herself. I put her on a large diet of pleasure. Bidet every day. Acknowledging her great life. Throwing a party for her friends. Bragging to her other Sister Goddesses. Re-creating her relationships with Annie and her other girlfriends, so that what they did with each other was brag about how well they were doing with men, rather than criticize themselves or each other. We got off the phone, Lucy hopped on the bidet, and wouldn't you know? Teddy called, asking her out. An hour later, they were at the car repair shop together. He helped her pick up her car, and they had a sexy, flirty "backseat of the car" date. Choosing fun is so powerful. You can't be in a relationship with a man, or a woman, without having your buttons pushed at some time or another. Mama is going to identify some hot spots for doubt and give you some alternatives to the swan dive.

Your Clock Is Ticking

Another area that is a particular hot zone of doubt for many women is the pressure of the biological clock. When a Sister Goddess starts to feel that pulsating panic that she should be married already or should be pushing a stroller by now, she may have a desire to revert to her desperate-to-get-a-man un-training tactics. This is a time to cling to Mama's training manual. During times of stress, S.G.s shouldn't change their approach to training but, if anything, should hold on to the principles even tighter. Trying to force a man into a husband suit because you hear that biological clock ticking won't shorten the process—it may well prolong it. Sister Goddess Barbara was on a tear. She had been desperately seeking a husband and a baby for ten years. She was twenty-nine years old, living alone in Upper Montclair, New Jersey, and feeling like maybe she was too successful to find a man. Or maybe she was too overwhelming or maybe she was too desperate or maybe she was desperate because her parents were so desperate. When she came to Mama, she was ready to try something new. I had her begin to study the discipline of pleasure. I had her go out with her friends for fun. She started to work out with a trainer. She decorated her apartment. She remembered she had a sense of humor. She decided, as she approached her thirtieth birthday, to ask her parents to throw her a big birthday party, with engraved invitations, since they would never get to give her a wedding! I suggested she register at Bloomingdale's for the gifts she wanted, and I bought her a subscription to *Modern Bride* magazine. Wouldn't you know, as she wriggled on the dance floor in her new toned and trained body at her birthday bash, she met Brad, the man who is now her husband. It's two years later, and they have their first child, a little girl. Sister Goddess Barbara's decision to have fun with her desperate circumstance created her dreams. Following your desires and pursuing your pleasure will bring any relationship to its strongest state fastest.

It's also good to remember that there are many other options available for a woman today who wants to have a baby. Check out Michelle Pfeiffer. She adopted the child that she wanted, then married the love of her life, David Kelley, and had another child. Calista Flockhart adopted her son and is now having a great romance with Harrison Ford. These women open doors for all of us to have our way in whatever way we want. If you want a baby and there is no interesting man in sight, look at other options. Remember, you're responsible for your own happiness.

He Thinks I Am Too Old and Fat

Sister Goddess Angela was married to a man who was twelve years younger than she was. She had been very happy for some time with her marriage and her life in L.A., but now she was feeling like she was too old for her husband, and wondered if he should be with a younger woman. Angela had met Frank at a time in her life when she was feeling fabulous. She had just become a Sister Goddess, she had received a promotion at work, and she had been dating up a storm. Frank was a makeup artist and was always working with young models and actresses. After they had been married a year or so, Angela decided that she was too old for him. She was watching him interact and flirt with a group of young women at a party, got jealous, and made a decision in her own head that Frank should be with a younger woman. She never told Frank of her decision, she just slowly withdrew from him. One night, as she was getting dressed to go to dinner with him, she said, "Do I look fat in this dress?" Frank hesitated for exactly one second before responding, and Angela burst into hysterical tears, collapsing on the bed, saying, "You think I am too old for you, and too fat, and you don't love me anymore!" Frank took her in his arms and tried to reassure her, but he could not penetrate her wall of doubt. They ended up separating, heading toward a divorce.

Angela took Mama Gena's flirtation class, as a little pick-me-up. She began to feel great about herself again, and she realized that she had been the one to disqualify Frank—he had not rejected her. She had fallen out of love with herself. That weekend, she had a bad fall and broke her arm. She really could not do a thing—not even the simplest task of washing herself. Her knight in shining armor, Frank, appeared. She was forced to allow him to serve her, take care of her, and do things for her. She began to really like him again. Frank had so much fun with Angela that he invited her to come to Europe with him on business. They are now in the midst of a delicious affair.

So much depends on our choice to love ourselves, rather than doubt ourselves! If you think you are too old, you are too old. If you think you are too fat, you are too fat. On the other hand, you can be eighty-nine and weight two hundred pounds on a five-foot frame, and if you think you are the hottest, sexiest, most gorgeous thing that ever lived, you are! Your guy will reflect your doubts and reflect your self-love with equal magnitude. Give him something wonderful to reflect.

He Would Never Go Out with Me

Well, that's a self-fulfilling prophecy. We are so in control of men, it's crazy. My friend Laura is a young woman in her early twenties who lives in Boulder, Colorado. She is gorgeous, always exquisitely dressed, made up, and coiffed. She is like a fragrant flower. She is in her junior year in fashion design school. I should mention that Laura is a paraplegic. She has no use of her legs, and partial use of her arms and hands. She is dating Randy, the cutest guy in her college. He is the only son of a wealthy Denver family, and he is absolutely crazy about Laura. He took her to her prom and lifted her up out of her wheelchair, and spun her around on the dance floor in his arms. If Laura had ever permitted herself to think she was disqualified from dating a guy because of her limitations, she would never be dating Randy. Randy never really thought he would date a woman in a wheelchair, he just found himself irresistibly drawn to Laura. You have the power to attract any man you wish. Just work it, Sisters. Turn those guys on just for the sheer fun of it. You will make his day—and your own.

It's one thing to doubt yourself, but what do you do when your guy gives you just cause to doubt him?

When He Goes Haywire

What's a Goddess to do when her prince turns temporarily into a frog? What's a Goddess to do when it seems her best-laid plans are starting to unravel? What's a Goddess to do when she is at the end of her rope of gracious adorability and is teetering on the brink of screaming maniac? How do we keep sight of our goals during times of stress and failure?

The highest state there is, in Mama's opinion, is the union of two different souls—a man and a woman, or a woman and a woman, or a man and a man. This union, especially when it's a man and a woman, is a union of differences. How do you make a union of differences? Any way you can. Use your powers of attraction, communication, and, if all else fails, whack him upside his hard head with a two-by-four. I can remember one night when I was angry with Bruce because he was not paying enough attention to me. I became so angry at his blunt insistence that he actually *was* paying attention to me that I screamed at him, "What color are my eyes?" He didn't know. "And how do I like my tea?" He had no idea. He was shocked by his own ignorance and woke up to new levels of attention, as a result of the whack from the two-by-four. Another time, I was so angry at him that I hurled a heavy glass right at his head. It was precisely aimed to whiz by his cheek and embed itself into the Sheetrock of the wall (do not try this at home). In the days, weeks, and months that followed, I would overhear Bruce proudly referring to this hole in the wall and telling guests the story of how I hurled the glass at him. The part of my anger that worked for him, and for us, was when I was demanding more from him or more for us, and volume was the only way I found to get his attention. He liked being directed to go higher. If I used my rage to put him down or insult him, it would not go well. He would get righteously angry and insulting and it would take us a while to recover the fun. Anger is so easy to get into and so hard to get out of.

Is There Ever a Time to Use Discipline?

S.G. Emily's fiancé Greg had a sensual encounter with the stripper at his bachelor party. Was this a reason to halt the wedding plans? Or was this just one more wild oat to sow before tying the knot? Mama will show you how to take control of the circumstances when all hell is breaking loose. This time that hell is a prince gone frog.

S.G. Emily had a great relationship with Greg, prior to the Infraction. They had been dating a year or so, and in that time, Greg had evolved from a party animal to a big sweetie. Before meeting Emily, he used to spend countless nights drinking with his buddies, picking up women, and playing a lot of racquetball and pool. After Emily, he gave up all those bad boys and bad habits and spent most of his free time with Emily. He was actually the last bachelor left in his group of guy friends. So when his bachelor party approached, it was only natural that his old abandoned pals wanted him to cut loose and go wild with them. In the heat of the moment, Greg was weakened by peer pressure and alcohol. Of course he told Emily about the Infraction the next day. She was pissed. Perhaps that is an understatement. Emily went wild when she heard what her big bad boy had been up to. She felt like dumping his ass, but she had a moment of sanity and called Mama instead.

I told Emily that the first thing we were going to have to do was some emergency spring cleaning. A high state of anger, no matter how justified, is no spot from which to make a decision that could possibly affect the rest of your life. Emily had to diminish her charge so she could see clearly enough to make relevant decisions about how to handle the Infraction. After she dumped a lot of her own charge on Greg, we talked about possible next steps:

1. Step into His Shoes. Even if you feel like throttling him, try to understand. Not to excuse, but try to see the situation from his point of view. Remember that he may have received bad training in the past. Consider what forces may have been in play that made him do what he did.

2. Stay, or Abort Mission. Ask yourself if you want to stay with the training. There are certain indefensible acts. The training project may be larger than you want to handle—only you can decide. In short, you should stay

as long as it's still fun, as long as you can stay in touch with your pleasure.

3. Lay Some Truth on Him, Don't Flush. Using your S.G. communication skills, let him know how profoundly unacceptable his activity was. Accept nothing less than what you wish for. Do this without crushing his spirit.

4. Consider *How Many Strikes Until He's Out?* This answer will be different for everyone. When you begin to lose touch with your sense of self and happiness, you may need to abort the mission.

Emily searched inside for what she wanted to do next. The wedding was a week away. She knew that Greg's old friends were pretty wild. In fact, she had not encouraged him to see much of that old crowd because she didn't like them very much. She realized, too, that if all the guys had been participating in the encounter with the stripper, it would have been pretty hard for Greg to refuse and keep his manhood intact. There were certain archaic expectations for the bachelor in his final moments of bachelorhood. And yet Emily felt she did not want Greg simply to be forgiven. She wanted him to experience some of the hurt and betrayal that she had felt. She and Greg came to see me. It was obvious that they were very much in love and wanted to be together and that Greg was full of remorse for his actions. We had to figure out some consequence that would make Emily feel better. Emily thought perhaps if she burnt Greg at the stake, it would cheer her up. I remembered the book *The Scarlet Letter*. In this novel, a woman who has committed adultery is forced to wear a scarlet letter on her chest as a form of punishment. I asked Emily if it would entertain her if Greg wore a scarlet letter to work for a few days. She said yes. We cut out a large red construction paper A and pinned it to Greg's sweater. He agreed to wear it nonstop for the next forty-eight hours or until Emily felt better. Greg was happy that there was something he could do to make both of them feel better. Emily was happy that Greg was willing to take this step. She felt like it was a way he could feel what she had felt. They agreed that if anyone asked what the letter was for, he would simply say, "It's a 'Scarlet Letter.'" He did not have to offer any further explanation. Emily also firmly explained to him that if he ever did anything even remotely like this again, she would not forgive him. She also knew that if she had not given her okay to the bachelor party, Greg would not have gone. He was not someone who needed to have time alone with his old buddies. And Emily knew she would have to pay more attention to whether or not she would want to see too much of these guys in the future. Probably not. This creative solution to their delicate situation was perfect. They both had a few good laughs over Greg's adventures with the Scarlet Letter, and they both learned more about each other. Their wedding was a few days later, and they had a glorious celebration and a wonderful honeymoon. They have been happily married now for four years, and Greg has never had another infraction.

It's easy to flush someone who has a misstep. When you feel

righteously angry, you can make decisions that have the potential to cut you out of some future happiness. Remember that training is a process, and if you are willing to keep checking inside to see what will bring you the most pleasure, not the most revenge or the most anger, you will always move in the direction of your goals.

Emily was able to go forward with Greg because he was exactly the right-size training project for her. Sometimes the training is much more than a gal wants to deal with. A stubborn guy can be entertaining, up to a point. It can be fun to crack a tough nut, but as soon as it stops being fun, it's time to move on. You are not a savior or redeemer. You do not want to change a man. And while you can teach an old dog new tricks, you do not have to. Pick a guy who is moving at a pace you want to go.

Sister Goddess Rita really wanted to get married. She was dating Arthur, who had dated her friend Lisa. They had broken up because Lisa could never get Arthur to commit to her. Arthur kept wanting to date other women, which drove Lisa crazy. When Lisa and Arthur broke up, Rita began to date him, thinking she could change him. If she was enough fun or sexy enough or generous enough, she felt she could turn him into her steady guy. Arthur had no interest in being anyone's steady anything. During this time, Arthur lost his job and Rita began to support him. She kept doing more and more for him, hoping he would change. It got so bad that Arthur's mother was telling Rita to break up with him, that he was no good and he would never change. His mother couldn't bear to watch Rita suffer anymore. Finally, Rita moved Arthur out and moved on with her life. Rita knew what she was getting into from her first date with Arthur, because she had watched her friend Lisa suffer through a relationship with Arthur. Arthur and Rita were at two totally different points in their lives. There is no point training someone who is not interested.

He Says He Will Never Say "I Do"

Sister Goddess Amy, age thirty, had been dating Ralph for a year, and every single time she brought up the subject of marriage, he screamed, "No!" Amy really loved this guy and thought she wanted to marry him. She came to Mama, almost desperate. When I met them both while they were taking one of my courses, I found out that Ralph had had a very unhappy first marriage when he was very young. He felt that he had been a failure as a husband. He loved Amy and didn't want to disappoint her or ruin their friendship and romance. All of Amy's friends were telling her to get out of that relationship, that Ralph was no good, not worth it, and she would be better off moving on to someone else. They all agreed that Amy was a great girl and deserved to be with someone who appreciated her.

My suggestion to Amy was that she have fun with Ralph. I told her that Ralph would end up marrying the woman who had the most fun with his resistances. It turned out that Amy had never had an orgasm. She found it hard to have fun with Ralph when she had a big area of doubt in her own life. She began to do some sensual training with Mama, starting with the "Demonstration of Extended Massive Orgasm" course with Drs. Vera and Steve Bodansky. After that course, she had her first orgasm, and Amy was off to the races. It was a huge boost to her level of confidence and, for the first time ever, she was able to flirt with Ralph while he was resisting her, rather than succumb to her own doubts. A woman can use a guy's doubt as a reason to aggress on her own fun. In fact, she has to. If she does not do this, it spells certain end for the relationship. Amy realized that Ralph's doubts were more about his own concerns and fears, and she stopped taking them personally. She was too busy exploring her newfound sensuality to be dragged to a doubt party. She also noticed that as much as Ralph protested, he was with her every night. When she became unexpectedly pregnant, Ralph proposed to her instantly and insisted on a huge, lavish wedding. Now he was calling the commitment shots.

But What If My Boyfriend Is a Control Freak?

I tend to think that we pick guys with dispositions similar to our own. If you think *he* is a control freak, it's probably because you are one, too. We are all control freaks. We want what we want when we want it. When you are single, this is easy to accomplish. When you are in a relationship with someone, it is not the most useful point of view. The most useful point of view is to hold two levels of awareness at the same time. Whaddaya mean, Mama? Decide that you are right and that your guy is right simultaneously. Two things can be true at once. When it rains on a day I have planned a picnic, it's bad news. But since we are in a drought right now, it's also, simultaneously, very good news. When you can find a way to get into agreement with whatever is happening in your life, you have found the keys to happiness, both with yourself and another person. It is only when we are in disagreement with what is happening that we are out of control. You can be in agreement with another person's point of view and still move forward on your point of view. When I moved in with Bruce, I knew that eventually we would move back into the city together. But in the meantime, I made sure I had fun in Great Neck. I painted our bedroom pink. I decorated. I got a job in a local restaurant and a teaching job. I baked, took exercise classes, and practiced training Bruce. I would plan things for him to do for me at night, when he came home from work. I was not accustomed to having a man in my life and I found it required a lot of planning to have fun with him. If Bruce had not offered to have me move in with him, I would never have had this wonderful time with him, in his home, with his family and his world. It was the best possible way for us to have begun our relationship. Give it up, gals. You don't have to work so hard to get where you want to go in a relationship. Let him do the work for you. He wants you to be happy and he will take you everywhere you want to go.

He's in Love with His Last Girlfriend

Guys are cute this way. They seem to have memories that are wonderful for recalling the good, and not as wonderful for recalling the bad. I can recount, in exquisite detail, the fights I had with Bruce over the last thirteen years, and he just remembers the good times.

This ultimately works in our favor. But if your guy is pining over his last girlfriend, you can sometimes feel vulnerable to doubt. The tendency is to feel that this means you are not as good as the last gal, but this is absolutely not the case! Fret not, just have more fun with him. He was with her longer than he's been with you. The longer you are together, and the more fun you have, the more his memories will fade and be replaced with hot, fabulous, delicious experiences with you. You could agree with him that she was the best thing that ever happened to him—after all, she gave him to you! Without her, you two might never have met. If you get angry at him or choose to doubt yourself instead of having fun, his last girlfriend will truly be the best thing that ever happened to him.

Have Fun with Your Desperation

Sometimes you will feel like you have done all the exquisitely good, hard work of exposing your desires, and you won't feel like your man is in any way responsive. This can really piss a gal off. It can feel like your worst nightmare. You have gone through this huge effort to spit out your desire, and he doesn't seem to have heard you. Or he doesn't acknowledge you. Or he doesn't take the action you desire. What now, Mama?

Before I met Bruce, I had created a big desire list, which hung on my refrigerator. The first item on the list was "To meet a guy so I can quit my job and marry him and have him support me so I can do whatever I want." And then I had about a hundred other things on my list. So when Bruce crossed my path, I was ready to quit my job and marry him and strike item one off my desire list. But Bruce was not rushing to Tiffany's with the same warp speed that I was moving. He was still trying to squeeze as much golf as possible in between dates with me. In my little world, I thought we should be spending weekends going engagement-ring shopping. I felt I was giving him all the hints he needed, I felt I was being suitably adorable. I felt that after dating six months, it was quite a respectable amount of patience that I had shown and now it was time for action. The operating pronoun in all my thoughts there was "I." "I" is good. It's the spot to start. But then we gotta consider the "him." The "him" in this case had never spent hours paging through brides' magazines while at the hairdresser. He'd never played bride as a child with his little boyfriends. He never went boyfriendless to family weddings or holiday parties. He just played golf and hung out with his pals, waiting for cute gals to walk by. My ego was in desperate need of a large diamond and a long white dress. His just wanted to have some fun and see what happened. What to do with all this conflict of interest? Easy. Bruce was not about to become as desperate or anxious about marriage as I was. It is a totally different experience for a man. Anyway, even if I succeeded in making him desperate, it wouldn't lead to fun. The only thing that would be fun for us would be if I lightened up and started to have fun with my overbearing enthusiasm for a diamond. It's fun or death in the world of relationships. Party with what's happening or the party will be over. The only fun way to make things happen in your world is through attraction. The only way you can attract is by relishing and enjoying your desires. It was up to me to dig down and party with my diamond desires, to make it fun enough for myself, and fun enough for Bruce to act on my desires. So I included my enthusiasm as a good thing. I decided to party with my diamond cravings, rather than repress, suppress, or deny my appetite. Whenever we took a cab to go downtown and passed Fifth Avenue and 57th Street, I would accuse Bruce of taking me past Tiffany's just because he was such a romantic fool who was trying to sweep me off my feet. Or when we walked past some jewelry store on our way back to my apartment, I would pretend to yell at him and tease him with deliberately trying to force me to look at diamonds when he knew I wasn't ready to make that big commitment yet. We got to laugh about My Big Appetite and enjoy it and use it as a way to grow closer. The inevitable thing happened as soon as we started to have fun. Bruce introduced me to his friend Hugh. Hugh worked in the Arcade Jewelry division at Sotheby's. Hugh suggested that we look at the diamonds at Sotheby's auctions. He said they were beautiful and you could sometimes find really great buys. Hugh took Bruce and me to the sale and, of course, there was The Ring. It fit me perfectly and was more beautiful than anything I could have dreamed of on my own. The next thing I knew, Bruce was sitting at Sotheby's, next to Hugh, holding his little paddle and raising it in the air as he bid against diamond dealers for my engagement ring. My warrior, going into battle for me. When we went to pick up the ring after the auction, Bruce got down on one knee, in the middle of Sotheby's, and proposed to me. That ring means so much to me, not just because it is beautiful but because it is a testament to the beauty of my desires.

Frogs Forever

There are some instances when, despite all of your best efforts, your prince remains a frog. When you realize that the training is no longer fun, that you are losing your sense of self, it's time to take a break and do something else or train someone else. You don't get any extra points for suffering. You don't get a prize for redeeming a loser. In fact, you can only train a guy who is willing and interested. Arthur was not willing or interested. He was far too self-absorbed ever to become a partner with a woman. You want to find a guy who has willingness. It's okay if his head is hard, but you want him to be at least interested in your point of view, in what you want.

Every woman has had a few incredible "learning experiences" with men. Even the most gorgeous, talented, sexy, successful women have had their share of hard-headed guys. Those of us who are interested in fun learn from our mistakes, rather than get stopped by them. I was reading a *New York Times* story about a heroine of mine, Halle Berry. She once had a boyfriend who beat her so badly that she lost 80 percent of her hearing in one ear. She divorced her first husband, David Justice, before marrying the love of her life, Eric Benet. "My divorce was so painful that I was forced to get the lesson because I didn't want to go through it again," she says. "I realized I had the power to choose a good mate—not be chosen, but to choose." Each of us has that power, the power to choose.

Warren Beatty had been really self-absorbed and rather disgusting before Annette Bening, but he became interested in her and in her happiness. As a result of her influence, he has matured into a very attractive man, both personally and creatively. Donald Trump was never interested in Ivana or Marla. He just wanted a pretty hood ornament by his side. A life-sized Barbie. Both those gals grew tired of his hard head and moved on. On the other hand, look at what Jennifer Aniston has done for Brad Pitt. He went from being a kind of androgynous boy to being a fun, interesting, artistically mature, sexy guy. Jennifer trained! So did Goldie Hawn. How totally attractive is Kurt Russell since she got her hands on him? Likewise Susan Sarandon and Tim Robbins. You can feel the fun that they have with each other. Their relationship seems really fun and sexy. It is such a pleasure to see a woman's influence on a man. Men always benefit from our influence. A man who has had close proximity to women is a more attractive man.

No woman wants to break through the layers of crust that can accumulate when a man is alone too long. That's why I think it is so important to train every guy we meet. Praise them for the stuff that works, tell them the truth about what doesn't. Yesterday I was shooting some segments for a TV show. The director, Che Che, could not have been nicer. He treated me like a princess, and I told him how much I adored that and how great that made me feel. On the set, I told him that if ever I got tense, he should say "pussy" to me, I would relax right away. He said it before almost every take, and we got all the shots in one or two takes. We worked beautifully together. My costar was a young kid of twenty-two. I went to use the bathroom after him and found the seat up. I said, "Darling, you have four sisters, how do you get away with leaving the seat up?" He explained that the girls were eleven, nine, seven, and five. I told him that a way to make them feel really special would be to put the seat down after he uses the bathroom. He was happy to find out that information. I love to lay a little friendly truth on a guy whenever I can. Another key principle in the training process: leave the guy better than when you found him. Leave him with more truth about women than he had when you met him. This is a gift to your Sisters. They will be the ones dating him next.

In this chapter, we will do some exercises that are surefire antidotes for the doubt and anger that can creep up on a gal as she begins the journey down the pothole-strewn highway called Training Your Hero. When a train derails, sometimes it's a problem on the tracks. Sometimes it's a malfunction of the train itself. We are going to look at how a Sister Goddess can manage to get her way, no matter what is going kaflooey. Mama will give S.G.s the tools to get that train—and herself—back on the tracks. Exercises will focus on reconnecting S.G.s with their desires and encouraging them to share their findings with their men. The more comfortable you become in exposing your desires, the less time you will have to waste in doubting yourself.

Exercise #1: The Nelson Mandela Exercise

Nelson Mandela is the person who is most single-handedly responsible for ending apartheid in South Africa. The way he did this was to stand up for his beliefs and hold on to his dignity, integrity, and love of humanity, despite the inhuman treatment that he and his people suffered. He never got caught in the crossfire of anger, and his love melted centuries of hatred and oppression. Is my example extreme? Yes and no. I figure if Nelson Mandela could find a way to tell the truth nicely and maintain the love in his heart, so can you. Sure, men are ignorant. Sure, they do things that are unkind or chauvinistic or uninformed. But we do not have to go to their level—we can bring them up to ours. Your job is to find a way to communicate your truth to a man, as though he were on your side and you were on his side. Be friendly. Be gracious. Tell the truth in a way that makes you feel good about yourself. Of course you want to be firm. Nelson was firm. I just want you to retain your integrity because it takes too long to recover from a bout of hostility.

True freedom is being able to take control of your world anytime, no matter what is happening. We will look at many different methods of having your way and gaining the support you desire from the men in your life. Remember, there is always a way for a true Sister Goddess to have her way. And having your way is the very best way for a man and a woman to spend their lives together.

Exercise #2: What Becomes a Legend Most?

Make a list of fantastically huge desires. For example, S.G. Felicia wanted to go around the world with her husband before she started a family. I just got a postcard from Marrakech. She is traveling for twelve months. S.G. Rene has a boyfriend whom she just adores. She had a fantasy that she wanted to fulfill—a summer in which she had a hot affair. Her boyfriend, Carlos, went on tour with a Broadway show and gave her permission to have a hot summer without him. She hasn't found anyone yet, but she is having an amazing time flirting her ass off. Most women only liberate their desires to the extent that they see other women liberate them. I am talking about really indulging the furthest reaches of your soul—becoming a legend. If Coco Chanel had not exploded past the barriers that existed in her day, we would not be wearing Chanel clothes or Chanel No. 5 today. Mama says you have a legend in you that is waiting to become legendary. Give it a voice. Then invite a man in to be inspired by your voice. Write your list of outrageous dreams, and then let your guys read it.

Exercise #3: The Approval Game

Approve of a man, just for fun. Do it deliberately, on purpose, and for your own fun. Don't go overboard with praise, just find a way to appreciate whatever he is giving you. Record this experiment in your journal. Notice what happens each time you appreciate him. You can pick any guy for this experiment—your boss, your brother, your boyfriend.

Exercise #4: The Doubt Your Doubt Game

It's very hard, if not impossible, to eliminate habitual behavior. The reason diets don't work is that we simply do not like having less.

Exercise usually works better because it's about having more. So, in this exercise, we are not going to try to eliminate doubt, we are going to do something better. Have your doubts. Give yourself a certain amount of time each day to doubt your head off. Let's say, from 10 to 11 A.M. Be deliberate. When you give yourself special doubt time, you will find that you probably won't be able to fill the hour. Also, you will be more entertained by it than victimized. It's kind of funny to give yourself a doubt hour. Another totally cool thing you can do is to doubt your doubt. You made it all up anyway, so you may as well doubt that your doubts are true, as long as you are in a doubting mood. Try it; doubting your doubt is better than doubting.

Exercise #5: Video of the Week

Watch the movie *Keeping the Faith* by Ed Norton. Watch as Jenna Elfman, who has fallen in love with Ben Stiller, makes the choice never to doubt herself or her love, even as Ben has a hard time committing to their relationship. Her love of herself and of him is what gives the movie its happy ending. If Jenna had ended up doubting herself, the movie would have had to have been retitled *Keeping the Doubt*.

Exercise #6: Photo Scrapbook Album of Your Brilliant Career with Men

Get a blank book. We are going to tamper with history here. I find that many women have been doing really well with the men in their lives, but they don't really admit that to themselves. Rather than being proud of every single guy they have dated, they feel they have fallen short because it didn't result in a home run. We are going to recondition you to look at every encounter you have had with a man as a delicious triumph, a wonderful learning experience, a fabulous memory, a great adventure. So you are going to create a photo album of all your great men. You can use their actual pictures or, if you don't have them, cut out a picture from a magazine that reminds you of your guy, or else make a little sketch of him. This is for your entertainment and self-celebration. I want you to use it the way people use photo albums of great vacations or stamp collections or a case full of gold medals. Your goal is to be proud of every one in your album, even if it's only one semimangy guy. When you start with pride, you will add on with pride. You can write a little if you want, a sentence or two on what was wonderful about him. You can date the pictures if you wish. Even if the relationship was stressful, it still brought you more of yourself and gave you a deeper understanding of who you are and what you want. We can find the good in everyone and everything. We are, after all, Sister Goddesses!

Chapter 8

Monogamy: Time for a New Model?

I think the reward for conformity is that everyone
likes you except yourself.

Rita Mae Brown

Okay gals, by now you have this training thing under control. I
know that "under control" is a relative term. The man/woman
game is still the highest-stakes game in the universe. Once you start
to play, every move in your life is a move in the game. If you are
happy that day, even if you don't see your guy, you draw closer to
him. If you are unhappy that day, even if you are nowhere near your
man, he feels it, and your unhappiness creates distance and discom-
fort in your relationship with him. A man is like an amplifier on
your life—he will amplify whatever direction you are heading. That
is why surrendering to your own happiness is so key. Since your
well-being controls the whole relationship, you all gotta surrender
to what it is that is ultimately going to deliver great joy to you.

Make sure that you are responsible for your own joy. You can't leave it up to anyone but yourself. You will want to, but it just won't work. Since a woman's desires sometimes scare her, this can be tricky business. For example, when I first got the idea in my head to pull Bruce out of his third-generation family business as a sales rep, I was scared. I thought, Oh no, his parents will hate me. His family will disapprove. What if we can't make a living? What will my family say? The desire was there, but I was scared of my own desire.

I want to open the doors for you to begin to entertain your desires. Invite those bad girls in and make friends with them and revere them and worship them and design your life around them. They will not look right, I promise you. They will look different from your mother's marriage or your sister's relationship life, or your best friend's affairs. Your design is your design. And since your design is your only shot at happiness, you may as well give in.

See a Brave New World

We have to look at the world that gave us the viewpoints we currently possess. Half of all marriages end in divorce within the first five years. You wouldn't invest your money in a fund that carried such risks. So what makes you think that if you do relationships in the way you were taught, it will turn out differently, or better? It will take more of you to give you more. If you were buying a dress or a house or a car, you would want to be the one to pick it out, wouldn't you? See, when our parents and grandparents got married, they did so for very different reasons than we do today. They married because it was expected, because of economic necessity, because of children. Today, you don't have to marry to put a roof over your head and food on the table. You can take care of your own fine self. You don't have to have children. There are plenty of people having children. You are still expected to marry, but you don't *have* to. It's not like it is the only choice. So why do people create relationships these days? For fun. For pleasure. To add to the quality of our lives. But you know what? We don't know how to create relationships for fun. We only know how to make the obligation kind. Because that's what our parents had. But, being women, we have a divine advantage. We have our desires. And our desires are a blueprint for fun. As long as we pay attention.

What is a successful relationship? It's a relationship in which everyone is happy and thriving. We have been conditioned to think that if we follow certain guidelines, happiness will result. But no one model will work for everyone, just as no one workout will work for everyone and no one diet will work for everyone. As a woman, it is crucial for you to follow your joy. There are different paths and trails to happiness in different relationships. The key is the same—a woman must get everything she wants. When the Mama is happy, everyone is happy. Right, darlings?

Choose to Be a Twenty-First-Century Courtesan or a Twentieth-Century Housewife

So let's loosen your joints about what is possible. For some women, a series of relationships with different great guys is a fabulous experience. This woman feels that "single" is not a waiting room, it's a destination. She loves being an adventuress on the open highways of romance. Then there is the serial marry-er. This gal has had a series of husbands, enjoying the temporary security of a marriage, the parties, and the variety. Then we have the woman who has her main squeeze, as well as a series of minor squeezes on the side. She loves having a long, intimate relationship with her man, with a little seasoning to spice up the mix. There is also the traditional monogamous woman, our one-man woman. And then there is the woman who is monogamous but flirts heavily as a hobby. There is yet another option that I want you to be aware of.

I want to invite you into the world of the courtesan, in this case, the courtesan for the twenty-first century. For centuries, successful courtesans were the most free women on the planet. From fifteenth-century Rome to nineteenth-century Paris, courtesans charmed Europe's most important leaders, seduced their way to power, wealth, education, and sexual freedom. They were the arbiters of style, fashion, and trends. Courtesans had the right to own property, to control their own money, to be educated, and to choose their lovers. They cultivated the Womanly Arts. This was a far cry from the other women, who had none of these privileges. Even noblewomen from wealthy families were considered the property of their fathers and husbands. They were denied all the freedoms we take for granted today. Actually, feminism arose because of the courtesan. Women saw the freedom that the courtesans possessed, and they wanted to experience that for themselves. The rise of the feminist movement in the twentieth century killed the courtesan. Feminism was achieved and expressed with anger, through the male paradigm of aggression, rather than through the feminine use of power. I read an article in the Style section of the *New York Times,* describing how high school girls are becoming the aggressors with the boys in their class. The girls are demanding dates and demanding sex from the guys. This is not a display of feminine power. It is a demonstration of girls imitating male behavior with the use of anger and force.

Feminine power is a very different paradigm. It occurs through attraction, not force or aggression. The girls learned from the men and the boys. I am interested in educating women and girls to use their power as *women* to conquer the world. It is much more fun. It feels delicious to everyone. And it is a much-longed-for voice, experience, sensation, and vista on this planet. We ache for the exquisite, pleasurable enjoyment of the power to attract and be attracted. Playfulness, rather than domination or submission. Unfolding, rather than knowing. The delicious languor of a well-played seduction, rather than the feeling of rushing or being rushed. Feeling, rather than accomplishing.

My definition of a twenty-first-century courtesan is this: a woman who knows and owns herself sensually. She lives via her desires, rather than her obligations or other people's blueprints for her. She explores the world with gusto, saying an enthusiastic yes to whatever she wants. Her pleasure is her first priority. She uses all the womanly arts—surrendering to her pleasure, having fun wherever she is, owning herself sensually, owning her beauty, flirting, loving her inner bitch, inviting abundance, and training her men.

She is aware of the privilege of being in her presence, aware of the impact of her beauty, aware of the radiance of her sensuality. She deeply appreciates the men and women in her life. She deeply appreciates and relishes every drop of her life.

Come, be a twenty-first-century courtesan with me. Take the time to let your desires rule your life, rather than let other people's opinions rule your life. Climb out of the box with me. That box you are in doesn't fit you, anyway. It never did. Find out what life your way looks like and feels like. Becoming a courtesan can take many forms. Experience the rush of freedom as a woman, as a courtesan.

Exactly what type of relationship is it that you want? Is monogamy your ideal, or are there variations on that theme that might suit you better? Is it reasonable for any of us to choose one partner to love, honor, obey, and have sex with for ten, twenty, thirty, forty, fifty, sixty years? Does the high divorce rate have anything to do with our culture's expectations for what a marriage is supposed to be? Do we have any other blueprints for a successful partnership that could include the possibility of wanderlust, or at least wanderlust in one's mind? Until the twentieth century, the courtesans defined freedom for women. They set the trends and standards of beauty and fashion. Using the example of the courtesan, we can research alternative lifestyles and partnerships between men and women. Mama will not prescribe any particular viewpoint, she will simply illustrate some alternative lifestyle choices that may perhaps stimulate your imagination. Mama is interested in expanding your worldview and giving you more than one way to consider partnership and love. She wants you to determine what relationship blue-print is right for you. Mama will show how this ideal can change as the circumstances in a S.G.'s life change.

When I first was dating Bruce, I was thirty-three years old and had never been married. I had been on a rather lengthy hiatus from men, and then I up and decided to get married. It was a race to the finish. Bruce, quite kindly, put the brakes on for me and suggested I date around a little before hurling myself into a lifetime commit-ment. While hating his idea at first I grew in time to so appreciate it. My idea of what it meant to be a girlfriend or a fiancée was that I sat around, waiting for my guy to escort me on appropriate dates. Bruce saw how I was diminishing myself and he suggested that, between our dates, I get myself out there and date other people. He wanted to make sure that I was not bowing to expectations, but, rather, bowing to myself. It was a bit of a mind-bending thought for me to date others as I moved toward marriage, but I had to admit, my pussy felt good about the whole thing. I remem-ber one day, I was having a tough time with Bruce, and I had a brunch date scheduled with a really nice guy. We didn't end up clicking, but he gave me some great perspective on men, made me feel beautiful, and I ended up introducing him to one of my girl-friends. I returned from the date happy, more in love with myself, and feeling closer to Bruce because of what he had provided for me, via the date with this guy. That is defensive dating.

I had other great experiences on my way to my marriage. I had several affairs, some romantic adventures, and generally sowed every oat that crossed my path. The cool part was that each of these experiences drew me closer to Bruce. He was the one man in the world who was offering me the whole world, including himself. Because I knew I had Bruce there by my side, rooting for me, grounding me with his love, I experienced sides of myself that I never could have experienced without him. I became more of myself with Bruce, not less. Our relationship was something that gave me more freedom than I had had as a single person, rather than being a noose around my neck, cutting me off from my desires.

How did I get Bruce to accommodate this side of me? By being willing to believe that it was possible that these desires were right, instead of wrong. Remember Violet who had an affair with her daughter's third-grade teacher? The difference between Mama and Violet, for example, was that Violet thought her husband was more right than she was. If she hadn't, she would have told him the truth rather than cheated. It takes a big leap of courage to jump out of the box that most of the world lives in and find that your desires are right. The rewards have been that Bruce and I have a relationship that is stronger, sexier, friendlier, and closer today than yesterday. It has been the romance of my life and the foundation upon which we have built our dreams.

Another Way to Have Your Way

Sister Goddess Patrice was married for fifteen years to a perfectly nice guy named Danny, and they had a son together and lived in a lovely home in New Orleans. Patrice just didn't do well in marriage. Marriage made her feel like a wife. She hated that. Being a wife made her feel like she had to do a whole lot of things that she had no interest in doing, such as making dinner and doing everyone's laundry. Patrice began to hate herself and her life. She separated from Danny and began an affair with a married guy named Anthony. This really suited Patrice. She felt a lot more comfortable being someone's mistress than she ever had being someone's wife. Being a mistress made her feel sexy and vital and alive. There were no dirty socks to wash, no dishes to do. It was all dinners out, hotel rooms, staying up all night making love and reading poetry.

But, Mama, I hear you shouting, "It's so immoral! And what about Anthony's wife?" Immoral is a relative term. What Patrice did was all aboveboard with open communication. She told Danny that the wife thing wasn't making her happy. He was informed of her every step, and they remained friendly throughout their separation. They share care and custody of their boy. As for Mrs. Anthony, she was interested in being married for many social reasons, but she had absolutely no interest in having sex or intimacy with her husband. They had married very young, had two grown children, and now had a nice friendship. Mrs. Anthony was actually relieved that Patrice appeared. Anthony was happier and he was busier, so he was off her back. Patrice was handling him sensually, so she felt relieved of her guilt over not being interested in him sensually. Mrs. Anthony felt relieved of her wifely duties. Patrice and Mrs. Anthony struck up a really nice friendship. The circumstances that they conspired to create made both women's lives a lot better.

This was not an easy decision for Patrice to come to. She had to overcome her own disapproval of her desires. She had parents who would have preferred for her to stay married. The same conventions surrounding her surround all of us. The difference was that Patrice decided to plunge into her happiness rather than compromise. The result was an extraordinary friendship between Patrice and her husband, Anthony, and Mrs. Anthony. Each of these people had an opportunity to create happiness and unprecedented partnership because of Patrice's courage. If Patrice had not gone for her desires, she would have been just another unhappy woman in the suburbs, quietly hating her life. Mama thinks we have quite enough of those, thank you.

Establishing Inventive Boundaries

Sister Goddess Wanda is a stockbroker who is married and has two small children. She is a wild, wonderful thing. She loves to have little sensual escapades with her girlfriends. Sometimes they go out to bars and kiss, sometimes they all get together and touch themselves and each other, sometimes one of their husbands will come along and watch. The deal with Wanda and her husband is that no other man gets to touch Wanda. She likes to fool around with her girlfriends but there are certain parameters that each of them observes to ensure the sanctity of their agreements with each other. Wanda and her financial analyst husband, Sam, are not interested in having Sam go outside their marriage for sensual experiences. They have found that Sam is turned on by his wife's occasional adventures, and that allows them both to have a little extra juice between the sheets. Another unique adventuress!

Sister Goddess Sandy is from the other end of the spectrum, but a courtesan, nevertheless. Sandy was in her twenties and divorced when she had a religious awakening. She became an Orthodox Jew with all the strict observances about the way she dressed, the way she observed the Sabbath, and the way she related to men. She began to look for a man who shared her religious beliefs and wanted to share this pathway with her. She dated many guys, met a widower with two teenage daughters who was a member of her synagogue, and married him. They have a beautiful life that includes family, observances of all the holy days, and a structured approach to the way they relate to each other as husband and wife. Sandy has never been happier. She counts on the rhythm of the holidays and her devotion to the faith she shares with her husband to bring her all the joy and gratification she ever wanted with a man. Sandy is a courtesan—a woman who takes deliberate control of her happiness and her relationship destiny.

Going Steady

Sister Goddess Cameron has been living with her lighting-designer boyfriend, Rick, for a year or so. She works at a public relations company. They have a great partnership and are very happy together. She recently met a guy named Harry whom she is very attracted to, and she developed a fun flirtation with him. She wants to date him. Cameron has two choices: she can give up the flirtation and resent her boyfriend for cramping her style, or she can make room in her relationship to explore this flirtation. Mama says, better to be inclusive than exclusive. If Cameron starts using her boyfriend as a reason to have less in her life, the relationship will be doomed. If she uses him to have more in her life, she has a shot not only at her happiness, but the happiness of the relationship. What woman wouldn't want to be with a man who wanted her to have everything and everyone she wanted? That's called having your cake and eating it, too. And having another cake besides.

Unlived life will get you. When a woman says no to one of her desires, everyone suffers. When a woman says yes to her desires, everyone benefits. And yes, I know, it is a radically different point of view to consider surrendering to your desires, but we are not doing too well with the denying-your-desires type of relationship. If Cameron said no to her interest in Harry, she would quietly blame Rick, grow to resent him, and gradually break up with him. By giving in to her desires for Harry, she can see what's there that attracts her, bring those good qualities into her relationship with Rick, and either get Harry out of her system or find out that she likes Harry better. Cameron shared with Rick everything about what she was feeling and what she wanted. Yeah, it could be a tough knothole for Cameron and Rick to get through, and they might not make it as a couple. But wouldn't you want your partner to choose you as the most fun and attractive of all the possible choices, rather than settling for you because it is wrong to be attracted to someone else while you are in a relationship? And by being friends and making room for each other during an experience like this, the potential exists for Cameron and Rick to draw closer to one another, rather than become enemies. When a man is willing to give a woman everything she wants, he becomes quite irreplaceable.

Friendship with the Alien

One of the factors that distinguished a truly accomplished courtesan was her ability to create friendships with the men she was with. Friendship is the absolute key factor in creating a cutting-edge, fabulous relationship with a man. If you can find a way to approve of every aspect of yourself, you can communicate about every aspect of yourself. We only keep secrets because we think certain thoughts or desires are wrong. No desire is wrong. They are all fabulous and they will lead to something wonderful. The trick of friendship is being willing to enjoy, really enjoy, and celebrate each other's differences, as well as the similarities. That is the heartbeat of a relationship. When you love the way *you* are, you can afford to love someone else. If you don't love yourself, you will simply accumulate reasons to disapprove of your partner.

Sister Goddess Tess is a well-known actress in L.A. She is thirty-four years old and has been dating Darius, a personal trainer, for a year or so. They each get a lot of offers for dates from other people. Before she was a Sister Goddess, Tess thought there was something wrong with her. She had been engaged to Walter, a nice guy from a very traditional background. Throughout their relationship, she had wanted to date other people but thought that was wrong. She tried to squelch that side of her personality. She wanted so desperately to be "normal." Then she met Darius. Darius seemed as wild and free as she wanted to be. They began an affair which led to the breakup of Tess's engagement. Tess did not want to continue hating that wild side of herself. She told Darius that if they started a relationship, she wanted to be free to be herself. She wanted to be able to flirt and experience everything that life had to offer. Darius was happy about this. He had always wanted a partner who would not restrict him, but challenge him. He loved watching Tess flirt with other guys. He encouraged her. He felt confident about himself, and he wanted Tess to feel confident about all of her desires. They became best friends, exploring the world of sensuality together. Tess had the experience of being able to be everything she is, with a man.

Darius encouraged her to explore. They would go to parties and make a deal with each other to flirt with as many people as possible, and watch each other flirt. They also planned little adventures, like experimenting with a threesome one night. This was such a new experience for Tess. She was able to tell Darius everything she wanted and have it add to their friendship and love. She had her best friend as her partner. She did not have to hide any part of who she was in this relationship. Tess was able to be responsible for her health and for Darius's health, because everything was out in the open with them. If they were planning to have an adventure, they would discuss exactly what activities they might like to engage in, and then what kind of protection they would use. They always used condoms, dental dams, and sometimes latex gloves to protect against any kind of venereal infection. This made everyone feel comfortable because there was minimum health risk. Everyone who partnered with them knew about their relationship with each other, so there were no expectations that the sensual explorations were anything but that—friendly adventures. It would not be pleasurable to sneak around or betray someone for a fleeting moment of lust. A courtesan of the twenty-first century wants an honest, true life.

Life, for many of us, is generously long. I hope that each of you, my courtesans, will have the gift of experiencing many sides of yourself in relationship. You may begin a relationship wanting to experience your wild side, as Tess did, and then you may evolve into wanting a more intimate affair with your partner for a while, and then, who knows what? The trick is to find yourself a partner to explore yourself with. If he is delivering to you the adventure of you, that is a gorgeous way to spend one's life.

Uniting the Differences

Sister Goddess Nora had been married for a few years to her best friend. They had traveled through Europe and the Far East and had recently moved back to Atlanta so they both could start new jobs—she in advertising, he in computers. As they put a deposit on their first house, Nora found out she was pregnant. She was horrified. It seemed to mean the end of all of her adventuring, all of her freedom, all of the possibilities that she had experienced. Ray was thrilled. He had always wanted children, especially children with Nora. The following week, Nora went on a business trip. She fell deeply in lust with Luke, a man she met in Montreal. She did not tell him she was pregnant. Feeling too guilty to do anything about her lust, she returned to Atlanta. She and her husband stayed up late into the night discussing what to do about the baby. Nora did not tell him about Luke. She said she wanted to terminate the pregnancy, perhaps separate. Ray was hurt by all of this, but he wanted her and wanted the baby. Nora made several appointments with the abortion clinic, none of which she followed up on.

The next month, Nora had to go back to Montreal again for business. She had been communicating with Luke via e-mail, and her lust for him was escalating. They met at a hotel and had passionate, crazy sex for a few days. By now, Luke knew of her pregnancy. It was all so wonderfully dramatic. When Nora returned home, she told Ray about her affair. He was devastated at first. Another all-night chat later, Ray decided that whatever Nora did, he still wanted her and the baby. He understood that she was overwhelmed at the thought of having a baby. She had been a foster child herself and was very scared about becoming a parent. He said he was with her, no matter what she wanted.

Nora had never experienced this kind of love before. She was more confused than ever. By now, she was in the fifth month of her pregnancy, still considering termination. She decided to go to Montreal again to see Luke. She discovered that he was having several other affairs with married women. It was a great way for him to have hot sex and no commitment. This was all Nora needed to come to her senses. She left that night for Atlanta and told her husband all that had happened, and all that she realized because of her adventure. She felt she really knew and experienced what love is, because Ray stood by her side as she had her affair with Luke. Here was a guy who adored her despite her fears, despite her betrayal, despite her lying to him. If a man could love her for all this, she had to consider herself one of the luckiest, most blessed women on the planet. Ray was grateful that she was such an adventuress, that she was so deeply herself, and so willing to share all sides of herself with him. They ended up having a beautiful baby girl and moving into the most loving, intimate, sweet side of their relationship. A true union of differences.

What's in It for the Guy?

So much. First and foremost, it is a privilege for him to be in your presence. Only a handful of men out there get to be with a woman who is happy. Most men spend their lives with women who hate them for not giving them what they want. Your man will be a man among men. We make men glad to be alive, but only when we are glad to be alive.

I have taken Bruce on so many ridiculously fun adventures. Once I had him fly to California with me for a day, just because I thought there was a course I wanted us to take together. But then I changed my mind and we flew home. But first we went to an orgy. I had him go to Paris with me to teach a course when I was seven and a half months pregnant. I had him take a lease on an apartment that cost three times what we could afford, but I believed in him, and he found the money for it. I had him take all kinds of wild sex and relationship courses with me, and get certified to deliver an Extended Massive Orgasm to a woman. I had him feed homeless people with me, drive a truck around Harlem delivering Christmas presents, stay up all night entering my last manuscript into the computer when I insisted on writing it longhand, and appear with me on a TV show that I wrote for us each week on Manhattan cable. I had him go snorkeling, learn to cook, diaper a baby, and take her to swimming lessons. I had him give up his career and join me in my adventure, setting pussies free. He has set up for countless courses, baked cakes for the different birthdays of the Sister Goddesses, done interviews for magazines, adopted cats, dogs, and turtles and taken care of all of them. I had him quit smoking, start exercising, and change his diet. Bruce has been pussified. And you know what? Five and a half years ago, when our daughter was born, he gave me a watch. The inscription on the back of the watch annoyed me when I first saw it. It said, "Desire Fun." I thought to myself, What does he mean by that? He wants me to have more fun desires? He wants me to desire more fun things than I desire? I was considering being insulted, but then I had the presence of mind to ask him what he meant. He said, "Your desires are fun." Oh, wow. That is so nice. My desires are fun. They really are. And he really thinks so. Wow. That is great.

Becoming a courtesan is taking a chance on love. It is betting the farm—on you. It is plighting your troth and plotting your course on the molten gold that lives within the deepest longing of your soul and the furthest reaching of your ecstasy. It is saying a nonnegotiable *yes* to the fire of your desire. It is the privilege and the opportunity to invite others, especially men, on your ride.

Exercise #1: Write Your Story

Write an essay on what it would be like to abandon yourself to your desires. To live with abandon. To surrender yourself completely to love. To become the heroine in your own novel.

Exercise #2: Lifestyle Q & A

Answer the following questions. They are nothing more, nothing less, than food for thought:

> Do you think it would be fun to be totally monogamous?
>
> Do you think it would be fun to be partially monogamous and have a few fun affairs?
>
> Do you think it would be fun to have a series of passionate affairs over a lifetime?
>
> Would you like to experience motherhood?
>
> Would you like to have a baby and have your husband raise it for you? Or with you?
>
> Would you like to live with a guy and have some kids?
>
> Would you like a man to support you?
>
> Would you like to support a man?
>
> Would you like to have a child on your own and have a series of lovers?
>
> How about several lovers at a time, all of whom contribute to your support?

These are simply thoughtful, provocative questions that will have you look at many different kinds of lifestyle choices in order to broaden the range of what you consider possible for yourself.

Exercise #3: A Tribute to Your Beauty

Inspire a man to do something extravagant in your honor. Raise him up out of himself, in tribute to you and your beauty. You don't really have to do much here except want it. This morning I was at Starbucks, in my usual leather chair, feet crossed on the ledge, facing the window. A man came by and bowed at my feet and kissed the window that my feet were pressed against. It was kooky, but I loved it. He must have felt I was writing about men serving women. I blew him a kiss, and he walked on, smiling. Sister Goddess Victoria just received a pair of five-thousand-dollar earrings from a man she just met two weeks ago. She actually has a boyfriend and the man who bought her the jewels is not dating her—he just wanted the privilege of being generous with her. Look at the Taj Mahal. Mumtaz Mahal was such a great inspiration to her husband, Shah Jahan, the Mogul emperor, that he built one of the Wonders of the World in her honor.

Exercise #4: Video of the Week

If you want a little inspiration in this field of inspiring men, watch the movie *Pandora and the Flying Dutchman,* with the incandescent Ava Gardner. In the first fifteen minutes of the film, she toasts marshmallows after an ex-boyfriend kills himself after she declines his proposal, then has her friend's boyfriend throw his race car off a cliff for her, and then she leaves him, tosses off her clothes, and swims naked to a yacht where she falls in love with the captain, who happens to be painting her portrait as she climbs on board. Ah, the sweet life of a courtesan!

Epilogue: Taking It on the Road

Plight your troth with your desire and you will inspire
a man for eternity.

Mama Gena

So, darlings, we've got you adoring yourselves, steering clear of doubt, asking for what you want, and communicating effectively. You are fully prepared for the grand experiment of having things your way and allowing your desires to guide your relationships. You've learned the Sister Goddess approach to relationships, which effectively turns on their heads the commonly held ideas of how to start and maintain relationships. Most important, you can see how "using" a man can take him higher than he's ever been, and keep a woman involved in a game that is truly worthy of her time and attention.

Women do not leave men who give them everything they want. Men do not leave women who use them. Men leave women who have stopped using them. A life of use can be the highest form of relating between a man and a woman. Coco Chanel had a hot, sexy boyfriend, Boy Capel, who was the love of her life. He invested in her business, put her on the map, and created her first couture shop for her. She used him well. Use can take many forms: sex, attention, food, shelter, clothes, shoes, jewels, adventures, travel, and so on. As women, we basically all want the same thing—we want everything we can think of and then more.

The way I see it, "using men" is either gonna be the sword that cuts you free in the world of relationships or the sword you impale yourself upon. Women's desires are the buried treasure of the twenty-first century. Buried for thousands of years. Talk about pirate booty. And the responsibility is ours, not our men's, to haul that gold bullion up to the surface and start spreading it around. Or, for the truly adventurous, you can teach your man how to scuba dive. Teach him how to go underneath the surface and explore your desires with you and how to encourage you to be true to what you want. That's a highly trained man. That's what I got going on with my husband. That's what I want for you. When he realizes that his great life is directly connected with the exposure of, and fulfillment of, your desires, you have some great adventure going on.

As you set off to train your man (or men), remember that training is not a solo activity. When I was single, I had a gang of pre–Sister Goddess girlfriends who were all interested in the same things I was, which is a great gift. We were up for including men, expanding our sex lives, having fun with guys, dating, that kind of thing. One or two of my girlfriends were married and wanted to have even more happiness in their marriages. The other three or four were single, like me. We would chat or meet regularly to discuss our progress. What helped me a lot was to use this group of girlfriends to keep expanding my fun. You will need a lot of reasons to quit being cranky and have fun with yourselves while cultivating yourselves. A group of Sister Goddess girlfriends is a great way to train yourself to train. Your first step is to make sure that the design of your Sister Goddess network is about bragging, discussing pleasurable activities, and adoring yourselves in each other's company.

Your Sister Goddess girlfriends are irreplaceable. I want all of you to have a group of women who support, sustain, and enhance your unfolding and their unfolding as women who get what they want from men. I do not want you hanging out with those man-hating types who have not yet kissed themselves awake. You want to be around women of like intentions. What do you think brides-maids are for? They are there to keep the bride happy, juicy, and feeling good so that, despite her fears, they can guarantee her voyage down the long white aisle to her dreams. And Mama's goal is not to get you married, it's to get you operational enough to get what you want. Get your Sister Goddesses together! It's not the prince who is going to be able to choreograph this waltz, it's going to be all on you, with the support and sustenance of your gal pals.

I never would have had the privilege of creating my prince or recognizing my prince without the incredible network of community that I have created in my life. I might never have ended up married to Bruce if my friends hadn't created such a smooth opening for us. Without the guidance of J.B. and Laura, and the constant love and inspiration of Vera and Steve, I never could have accomplished the things that make me proudest—my love affair with, and recognition of my love affair with, Bruce. And as I look back on our romance, I see that it has always been so.

You can always bring your friends into the game to assist you. Sister Goddess Susannah wanted a pretty watch for her fifth-anniversary present. She had taken Steve shopping and they had seen the watch she wanted. She had clipped out a picture of it from a catalogue and taped it to the mirror above her dresser. Her fifth anniversary came and went, and no watch. Susannah was very disappointed. Mad, even. She felt that the watch, while expensive, was within Steve's grasp. She felt she had left a suitable trail of crumbs in his path. She could not understand why he had not delivered.

Fortunately, her birthday was just around the corner. Sister Goddess Rachel was also in Susannah's class, and her husband, Allen, was friends with Steve. Mama suggested that sometimes a little team tackling is in order since the smoke signals had not been detected. Rachel enlisted Allen to help the cause. The next time the two guys got together for racquetball, Allen asked what Steve was planning for Susannah's birthday. He said he hadn't really been thinking about it. Steve just wasn't one of those big holiday planners. Allen told him how much Rachel loved it when he did something extra special for her birthday. He asked if there was anything that Susannah wanted for her birthday. Steve said he didn't know. Allen said, "Didn't you two go watch shopping a few weeks ago?" This was enough to jog Steve's memory. He remembered the photo of the watch taped to Susannah's dresser. He thanked his friend Allen and off he went to the store. Susannah got her birthday surprise, and Steve got to be the hero of the day, with the help of his friends. And it's not even the watch that is all that important. It is not the cost of the gift, either. It is his exquisite attention that creates the magic.

esire is all. It is the heartbeat of the universe. The life force. The throb, the pulse that causes being. You are empty without it, abundantly lush with it. Desire is the most powerful, sustaining, creative force on earth. Desire is a direct-access pipeline to the Goddess, the divine within, that which is greater than ourselves. It is like possessing the source to life. Desire is the delicate, eternal interface between human and divine. When we create space for desire to flourish, we invite Grace to sit by our side and guide us to a place far greater than we could conceive on our own. True desire is not about ego. It is about listening, paying attention, and cultivating the voice within. Surrendering to desire is the most courageous, adventurous, spiritually exalted way to live one's life. Men do not have desire. They respond to our desire. Women do not yet really know the exquisite value of their desires, and men do not yet know the importance of paying attention to women's desire. That's okay. The adventure of a man and a woman—creating union, based on both of them surrendering to her desire—is the next frontier. That is a life worth living, a relationship worth having. For her, the adventure is learning to value, give voice to, and share the most precious part of herself that she has sealed away. For him, it is about taking his attention off himself, and putting it on her, for the sheer joy of it. We can all learn to go gold prospecting together. We can each sift through the sand for a little gold dust, a little nugget, and then before long we will have a hot, throbbing desire that is worth its weight in gold. And the exalted adventure that unfolds when a woman and a man surrender themselves to her desire is spectacularly miraculous in its divine consequences.

About five years ago, I had unexpected lust for art explode inside me. I love real paintings, done in real time. Specifically, I had a picture in my head of a portrait of me, hanging over the fireplace in the living room. Bruce and I had just moved into the brownstone, tripling our rent, and our daughter was barely a year old. This was a time to figure out how to make the rent payments and keep food on the table. This was not a time to be collecting art. But I could not stop the desire. I kept seeing the portrait presiding over the room where I teach. I felt so strange about this. I did not want to want it. I wanted to ignore it, to be more practical. I hesitantly told Bruce about it, and he said, "What! Are you crazy? We can't afford that!" Interestingly enough, though, he immediately had ideas on how to make it happen. He suggested that a client of ours, a well-known portraitist, might be interested in bartering with us.

I had just begun my Mama Gena 101 class, and I wanted the portrait to be me, as Mama. Bruce encouraged me and sat with me as I talked to the painter, who agreed to barter with us. I was thrilled and nervous. But, then, I felt suddenly too selfish or self-important to go through with this. Especially because the artist asked me to wear something wonderful to get the portrait done. Wonderful? I had nothing wonderful. My closet was filled with mommy clothes or maternity clothes. I didn't have any money for clothes. I never really allowed myself to think about what Mama Gena would wear. I only knew I had nothing in my closet that she would even consider. I froze. It was the morning of the day of my first sitting and I had nothing to wear. I tore through my closet with my friend Karen, and we both agreed that there was nothing. Bruce suggested that I stop at Bergdorf's on my way down to the studio to pick up an outfit. He had never been there, he had just heard of people buying lovely clothes at that store, and for some reason, we had gotten a Bergdorf's credit card, which we had never used. He gave me the credit card. Now, I had never been to Bergdorf's. I went with my friend Karen who had shopped there before. I immediately felt that I was in over my head. It looked more like a museum than a clothing store. My pal Karen guided me to the second floor, where designer clothes were housed. I was queasy and wanted to leave. Karen dragged me around. I insisted on only looking at sale items, which were all too expensive, anyway. Karen told me to shut up and she put me in a dressing room and insisted that I try on a Mary McFadden dress. I had never seen anything like it in my life. It looked like something that someone would wear to the Oscars. The top was totally beaded and off the shoulder. The beads looked like jewels. The bottom was a wonderful aqueous green Fortuny fabric that dripped onto the floor. It was something a Goddess would wear. I looked so beautiful, and so Mama Gena. The feeling of being in this dress was remarkable. It was elevating and comfortable and so glamorous. Karen insisted I buy the thing. She said I could sit for my portrait in it, then return it. I was paralyzed. It cost six thousand dollars. I had never bought anything for that much money in my life, much less a dress.

I called Bruce and told him about the dress and Karen's buy-and-return plan. He heard the extreme nervousness in my voice. He reassured me to go for it. "It's an adventure, and you are worth it, especially since you can return it tomorrow!" I can still remember the totally keyed up, swirling, nauseated feeling of standing at the register. Karen suggested I split the cost between my Bergdorf's card and my American Express card, since neither contained enough credit on their own. I was feeling for sure that my cards would be declined, that I would be found out as a fake. I literally shook as I signed the sales slips. And then the feeling of getting into a taxi, carrying a six-thousand-dollar dress! It was an out-of-body experience. I thought for sure I would get robbed, that people could see that I was out of my league. How do you hold a shopping bag that has six thousand dollars worth of contents? When we arrived at the artist's studio, a lot of people were there. The artist's sisters, who had all taken my classes, were in town. They asked me to put on the dress. It was magically beautiful. They all encouraged me by saying that I looked wonderful and had done exactly the right thing. Because they expected me to be able to handle this dress, and have such a dress, I was able to fake my way through. Inside, I was still in shock, wondering if I had gone mad. I put tissues under my arms so I wouldn't sweat in it. I sat cautiously so as not to wrinkle the dress. I did my best to become a living hanger to display this beautiful dress. Bruce called me. Did I get to the studio safely? Yes. Would I please be careful not to get any paint or anything on the dress and not to sweat in it. I told him about the tissues in my pits and told him how nervous I was to even be wearing such a dress, even for a few hours. He called back a little while later. "Do you love the dress?" Yes, I said. "Do you want to keep the dress?" No, I said. It makes me too nervous. "Okay, but you deserve the dress. You are so beautiful, you deserve a six-thousand-dollar dress. If you want that dress, you are going to have it." He seemed moved and fortified, like Shakespeare's Henry V, heading into victorious battle. "Thank you, but no way," I said, then hung up. An hour later, we finished the sitting for the day. I looked at the portrait. The painter has outlined the face, and done the eyes. I was crestfallen and terrified. I was not due to return to my second sitting for another week. There was not one drop of the dress in the portrait. Not an outline, not a brushstroke. The doorbell rang. It was Vincent, a friend of mine who is a stylist and artist, who knew I was having my first sitting that day. I blurted out the whole story to Vincent, choking back my tears about the dress. When I told him that Bruce just called and offered me the dress, and I declined, he was horrified. "You must accept!" he said. "You are Mama Gena. Mama has clothes like that. Your husband offered to buy you a six-thousand-dollar dress. You don't want to insult him! And that's not all. You have to wear the dress, the dress cannot wear you. Each time you come for a sitting, you have to come in a town car, not the subway or taxi. You must wear the dress in the car, on the way downtown. Learn to walk in the dress, sit in the dress, recline in the dress. You have to get the right shoes and underwear. Live into the dress. Make it your own. Say yes! to the dress." I can't, I thought to myself. It's too much for me. I can't even afford the underwear, much less, the dress. When Bruce called back a few moments later, I told him the whole story. He said, "Vincent is right. I don't care what it takes, I am going to buy that dress for you. I am going to make sure you ride in a town car and wear the right shoes. You go for it, baby." I went home, shell-shocked. All these people were pushing me, shoving me, pressing me into my dreams. Imagine. Bruce, who struggled to pay our rent, who was just acclimating to fatherhood, wanted me to have this extravagant gown. It was a lot to absorb, a lot to say yes to. But if I declined, I would be telling him that I didn't think he was up to the challenge, that he wasn't man enough to afford a six-thousand-dollar gown for his wife. I was always telling women that their dreams are not too big for them, that everything they desire is possible. I had to say yes.

So I kept the dress. I went to all my sittings in a town car. I learned to wear just the right makeup, jewelry, shoes, and underthings to feel amazing in the dress. I practiced walking, lounging, sitting. One day I even wore the dress to fold laundry, just to see how it felt. I got better and better at feeling comfortable in finery. I even went on some special Mary McFadden list at Bergdorf's and got invited to a private fashion show at the store. And, yes, we went into debt over this dress. We lost our American Express card because of insufficient payments, and we were late paying other bills. We had to really kick some butt to stay afloat. But you know what happened? Mama Gena unfolded. I invented new classes, I did speaking engagements, I wrote my first book, I was invited to appear on television. Articles in national magazines were written about us. The dress drove us all higher—keeping Mama afloat was a huge responsibility. And it was hugely attractive to people. It was almost like everyone in my world, not just Bruce, was responding to my desire to create Mama and the School of Womanly Arts. We were living the razor's-edge life, perilously close to financial insolvency, and yet miracles happened at every turn. We had volunteers training with us, so we didn't have salaries to pay. Once, one of our volunteers paid our rent for the month. A client threw a fancy party for us. Suddenly, designers were giving *me* clothes to wear at my appearances. My wardrobe was starting to look like the wardrobe of the woman who owned that six-thousand-dollar gown. Vincent's admonishment to me to live that way had come true. Because of Bruce, I owned that gown. Because he trusted that the woman he loved was a star who deserved such an extravagance, I had become one.

And that is the kind of adventure that is possible when a man and a woman surrender to a woman's desires. Thousands of men and women have benefited from my selfishness and Bruce's devotion. And the entire experience has been so much fun. Our lives have been filled with great romance, heartbreaking devotion, terror, huge obstacles to overcome, fantastic triumphs, shocking disappointments, travel, adventure, ridiculously fun sensual adventures, and enormous love. Because of Bruce, I have become every drop of the woman I was meant to be, and because of me, he has become the hero he never had a shot at being, without me. It is fun to live the stuff of legends. Go on with you, then. Become the legend *you* were born to be. And remember, Mama loves you.

About the Author

Regena Thomashauer (Mama Gena), creatrix of Mama Gena's School of Womanly Arts, is an icon, a movement, and a revolution rolled into the body of one hot woman. She is a woman who has the courage, passion, tenacity, and enthusiasm to actually live her dreams. Regena graduated with a B. A. in Theater Arts from Mount Holyoke and then retired from the stage to pursue her "exhaustive" research into pleasure and fun. She has dedicated her life to researching the nature of pleasure, specifically female orgasm, and its relationship to health, well-being, and overall fulfillment. She is certified to teach courses in extended massive orgasm. Regena is self-educated in the history of women—socially, culturally, and economically—and is an expert in the anthropology of the ancient Goddess religion. She uses this research to open doors for women today by giving them a context in which to maximize their actual power, passion, enthusiasm, and creativity. She lives in Manhattan with her husband, Bruce, and her daughter. To learn more about Mama Gena, please visit *www.mamagenas.com*.